THE POPPA
and the
PUNKIN

A WWII ROMANCE TOLD IN LETTERS
(1939-1946)

TIM DUNN

Print ISBN: 978-1-09831-500-9

eBook ISBN: 978-1-09831-501-6

CONTENTS

PREFACE

SOON AFTER DAD DIED TRAGICALLY OF A HEART ATTACK IN
June 1964, Mom, my 17-year-old brother Chris, and I (Tim) begin cleaning
out our basement in our suburban home in New Jersey. Among the many
boxes, we discover one that contains stacks of letters written between our parents from 1939 to 1946, from their courtship to his return from the Pacific
theatre. Interspersed among these 600 letters were about 50 letters from
Dad's mother, Leonora, to Dad from his 1942 entry into Officer Candidate
School (OCS) until his return Stateside. There are also a number of letters
from Mom's brother, Bill, to her, written from the European front during the
last six months of the War, from the Battle of Bulge past VE Day. There are
also sporadic letters from other family members, aunts, uncles, and cousins.

With the pain of Dad's death shooting through her, Mom's immediate
reaction is to tell my 17-year-old brother and 14-year-old me to not look at
any of the letters and tape up the box. She is 49 years old and for the next 36
years, far longer than her 24-year marriage to Dad, we were not aware of her
ever opening this painful Pandora's Box. Who knows, she may have looked
at the letters. My parents' desire to save all these letters is documented in one
of Mom's letters with their expressed hope to share them in a retirement that
never happened.

The box was carried from our family home to a new house and when
Mom decided to move to Boston to an assisted-living center near our home;
the box was stored unopened in our basement.

Mom died of complications from a stroke in 1998 without ever dating
another guy or telling us many stories of her relationship with Dad before we

were born in 1947 and 1950. As my brother and I move toward and past 70 years, maybe it's time to share the mysteries of the letters. The story begins:

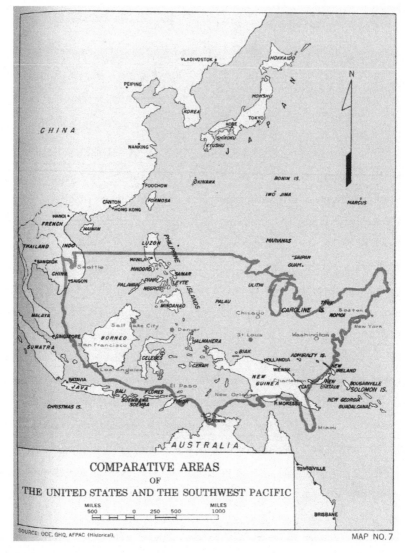

This 1940's map of the Pacific Island chains used on the book cover was chosen for specific reasons. First, the red outline of the United States shows the vast geographic area of the US superimposed over the even larger area of the Pacific islands where the Allies were in combat with Japan during WWII. Imagine the area that US forces had to cover. Secondly, our Dad, Major Don Dunn, was flown over 2000 miles per week for one year to inspect and investigate safety, supply and logistical support problems that were absolutely required for the US in their defeat of Japanese forces. Dad earned his frequent flyer miles in this vast area in an Army Air Corps DC 3 at 7,000 feet above the endless Pacific.

INTRODUCTION

AFTER I FIRST READ THE LETTERS DURING THE SUMMER OF 2019, I began to review memoirs of people who faced the loneliness and horrors of WWII. Most of the memoirs were based on letters from one military person to a loved partner or family member. I realized how our collection of correspondence was quite unique: a dialogue between Mom and Dad, a dialogue between Dad and his mother, and a dialogue between Mom and her baby brother. A family sharing its stories of WWII.

The Poppa and The Punkin: A World War II Romance Told in Letters (1939–1946) describes the following:

- An eight-year dialogue between Mom and Dad, from their courtship in '39 to their reunion at Philly's Sheraton Hotel in April '46
- An almost daily exchange of letters over a 12-month period when Dad was in Hollandia, Dutch New Guinea, and Manila, Philippines, serving as a traveling major for the Inspector General's office, while Mom lived in Pennsylvania with her family
- Mom's brother Bill's letters from the European front; written between 1944 and 1945, from the Battle of the Bulge past Berlin, they are the words of a 25-year-old private to his older sister with whom he could tell his darkest fears and brightest hopes.
- A slice of Grandmother Leonora Dunn's letters to her son, Donald, our Dad from 1942 to 1946; sadly, most of these letters did not survive the jungle environment of the South Pacific. Only our grandmother Leonora's letters that Dad included with his letters to Mom were saved.

- One additional stroke of luck was that in Dad's year-long sojourn abroad to the Pacific, Mom traveled to New London, CT, from Pennsylvania for a three-month-long summer visit to Dad's family. There are a number of letters from my mom that describe what was happening on the home front in Dad's family: selling the family home, the death of Dad's grandfather, the failing health of his own Dad, the growing economic strain, and the joyous wedding of our Uncle Ned to our Aunt Maud, which Mom helped orchestrate.

Our parents spent great effort keeping track of their correspondence sent 10,000–13,000 miles across the ocean. Each of the letters was numbered. Each time our parents would write, they would enumerate the letters they had received. Dad would even mention how many letters he had received from his mother, probably equaling Mom's 300 letters. Mom would share her brother's letters with Dad.

We have a record of our family's letters to each other, which describes their reactions and feelings about this global conflagration. They record their emotional reactions to the events of the Second World War: its beginning in September 1939; the shock of Pearl Harbor in December 1941; the months of our parents' separation in the US from June to December 1942; three years of moving together from Enid, OK, to Garden City, KS, to Waco, TX, to Salt Lake City, UT, from December 1942 to March 1945; and when Dad shipped off to Hollandia, Dutch New Guinea, and Manila, Philippines, from March 1945 to April 1946. Their joys, grief, sadness, anxieties, fears, loneliness, and aspirations for the future tempered by their ceaseless worries and their truly ecstatic moments when Poppa would get a letter from the Punkin or Punkin would hear from Poppa.

During that year in 1945–1946, the family, like other Americans, faced the devastation of Roosevelt's death, thanksgiving for VE Day, the family's fear of our traumatized uncle being shipped to the Pacific to attack Japan, their differing reactions to the atomic bombs in Hiroshima and Nagasaki— VJ Day, the creation of the UN, and their eight months of frustration, separation, and loneliness until Dad's and our uncle's return Stateside in April 1946.

Their stories are important to tell in their own words, as they reflect what so many other American families experienced during the war.

Why another memoir of World War II? First, this Summer we commemorate the 75ᵗʰ anniversary of the War's end and the creation of the United Nations. Although the UN has not stopped all war, it has been the means to prevent nuclear disaster and a repeat of the violence of WWII. Secondly, the US Department of Veterans Affairs determined that around 16 million US men and women served in World War II. By September 2019, only 375,000 of the 16 million were still alive.

Today, their death rate per year is well over 127,000 men and women, sadly and ironically exploding with the birth of Covid-19. By 2023 or probably much sooner, we will face the sad reality that the "Greatest Generation" will be gone.

Thus, this memoir shares the stories of the Greatest Generation, all our parents—that many of our own generation, we "Baby-Boomers" do not really know the details. Whether it be from their early deaths or painful memories too difficult to share, we boomers may not understand some of our own beginnings or shared values as we begin to face the closing chapters in our own lives.

The Poppa and The Punkin: A World War II Romance Told in Letters (1939–1946) may open up some important memories for all of us.

One final note—the title of the book originates from the nicknames that my parents gave each other sometime early in their marriage. Dad became "Poppa" and Mom became "The Punkin" sometime during the early years of their marriage. So, you will see these nicknames throughout the book, especially after Dad leaves for the Pacific. Enjoy the stories of The Poppa and The Punkin with occasional appearances from Grandma Leo (Dad's mom) and Uncle Bill (Mom's only brother).

The Organization of the Book

The first section of each chapter will describe the narrative of what is happening in Mom and Dad's lives during the time frame of the chapter.

The second section of each chapter will be the letters Mom, Dad, my grandmother, and my uncle sent to each other during the time frame of the chapter.

The major events and battles of WWII will be interspersed among the letters to provide a timeline and context for the family's letters in each chapter.

Family members mentioned in the book: If you get lost, come back to this chart to get a refresher.

The Dunn/Fones Family—Dad's family

William Alonzo Fones, our paternal great-grandfather

Leonora Fones Dunn and Herbert Luther Dunn, our paternal grandparents

Their children, Dad (Donald Elton Dunn or Poppa) and Uncle Ned and Uncle Herbie

Dad's aunt and uncle, Byron and Arlene Fones

Dad's first cousins, Alma Fones (her husband, Ed Eshenfelder), Jack Fones

Maud Sullivan Dunn and Abbie Dunn, Mom and Dad's sisters-in laws

The Schuberts—Mom's family

Danielle and Walter Schubert, our maternal grandparents

Their children, Mom (Jeanne Schubert Dunn or The Punkin) and my uncle, Bill Schubert, Shubie-puss

The Donald E. Dunns, Jeanne and Don—Our parents

Their sons, Chris, my older brother, and Tim, myself

PART I

Love and Marriage Under the Shadow of War

CHAPTER 1

Family Roots

(DAD, DONALD ELTON DUNN: 1907–1964)

THE POPPA

DAD WAS THE PRODUCT OF A MIDDLE-CLASS FAMILY IN NEW London, CT, with English and Irish immigrant roots back to the eighteenth century in Rhode Island. Born in 1907 to Herbert Luther Dunn and Leonora Fones Dunn, Dad was raised in a busy household. His dad was educated as an engineer at Brown University, and his mom's family had a successful marine building and salvage company that built many of the lighthouses dotting the Connecticut coast on Long Island Sound. Dad grew up in a large Victorian with his parents, his mom's parents, a couple of his dad's maiden sisters and his three brothers, Kendall, Herbert Fletcher, and Edward "Ned." For 30 years, they had a "colored" cook and maid, named Fanny, who came in two days per week, and was an important part of the family.

Dad's childhood was comfortable and happy: He was a paperboy. He attended New London's First Baptist Church, where his mother got him involved with various theatricals. With adolescence beginning, he was enrolled in a private boy's day school in New London. At the Bulkeley School, he clearly came into his own: Playing leading roles in Gilbert & Sullivan and Shakespeare's comedies and tragedies and acting as the head cheerleader for the boys' sports teams, he sounded popular yet sensitive and romantic. His yearbook bio described these characteristics: "Dunnie is so cute, sweet and kind that all the girls seem to fall in love with him but how will he ever choose one!"

One letter written by Dad from Hollandia in Dutch New Guinea in 1945 painted his own picture of growing up in his middle-class New London family. (Mom was spending that summer of 1945 with his family.)

DAD WAS A NEWSBOY FOR
THE NEW LONDON DAY.

DAD'S HIGH SCHOOL
YEARBOOK PICTURE

Thursday, July 5, 1945
Dutch New Guinea

Darling,

. . . Someday I shall tell you of my youth. I shall start now. I was hopelessly romantic. I fell in love completely, utterly, despairingly. I soared and I was plunged into depths. I saw a grammar schoolgirl at a grown-up play rehearsal that I was in. She was partially undressed in a scene where she was being put to bed. I fell in love with her petticoat and the girl, too. It was more than a year later as a freshman in high school, I met her at dancing class and burst forth this first distant love into a flaming romance (on my side) which lasted with devotion for three years, three long years. I would walk my paper route a different way each Tuesday because at 5.30 p.m. every Tuesday afternoon

she would finish her piano lesson at one of my customers and so
promptly at 5.30 p.m., I would deliver the piano teacher's paper,
to walk my swain to the trolley. One hot summer day, probably
about 1923, I ran. I ran all the way from Ocean Beach to Willets
Ave (Dad's street) to be with her as she rode her bicycle. Love, D.

IN 1925, HE WENT OFF TO THE WHARTON SCHOOL AT PENN
to study economics. Home for the summers, he hung out with his brothers,
his first cousins, and his New London friends, going to the beach daily after
finishing work at the Lighthouse Inn as a bellhop.

Although his college education was initially paid for by his family,
during his last two years and some years after graduating in 1929, he had a
full-time job as a manager of a Childs Restaurant at 18th and Chestnut in
Philly at the beginning of the Depression.

He finally landed a job with the large brass manufacturer, Scovil, which
took him to Bridgeport CT., Pittsburgh, and Cleveland for almost 10 years.
He was let go in the economic downturn of 1938, which, by his own admis-
sion, caused a major crisis of confidence. But he did not immediately look
for another sales job. The life of a corporate Willy Loman had lost its appeal.

The corruption and failures of state and city governments had been
apparent in the US for some years, and piqued Dad's interest. The improve-
ment of local and state governments drew him back to Wharton School at
Penn where an institute to improve local government was created. The political science minds of the 1930s concluded that the solely political model of
towns and small cities was not served by a system of only elected mayors, town
councils, or town meetings. The job of running a town needed to be profes-
sionalized, and a new career was created: town administrator or manager.
Elected officials would continue to oversee this process, but a professional
with the business, financial, and technical skills would lead daily operations.
Dad was one of the first graduates with a Master's in public administration
from the Fels Institute of State and Local Government at Penn in the winter

of 1940, having just completed his internship in the Department of Public Instruction in Harrisburg, PA.

This serendipitous placement changed Dad's life forever.

MOM, JEANNE SCHUBERT DUNN: 1914–1998

THE PUNKIN

MOM'S CHILDHOOD COULD NOT HAVE BEEN MORE DIFFER-ent than my Dad's. The daughter of Polish immigrants, she was initially raised in Wilmerding, PA, the home of Westinghouse Air Brake. The entire Monongahela Valley was filled with steel mills and factories all powered by coal. Everything was full of dirt and coal dust.

Her father, Walter Schubert, had come to the US with some skills. He spoke and wrote fluent English. He became a leader in the émigré community, making his money by selling insurance to many of the other immigrants. He had also started a notions store.

With his income, he was able to buy a house in Wilmerding, PA, in a middle-class neighborhood. However, his dirty, sad secret was that he was a gambler. Before the Depression even started, he had lost everything, including the family house. The family had to move in with our mother's grandparents in a town nearby. The only space available was in the attic where Mom and her brother spent most of their childhood and adolescence, bunking in with their parents.

Although Mom and her friends were financially compromised, they attended high school, got involved in activities and sports, and dated their football heroes, graduating in 1932 at the height of the Depression. Mom was determined to get out of this depressing environment and worked as a secretary at the Air Brake for two years to save money for Temple University in Philadelphia, where she had been accepted. She had to live off campus as an 'au pair' and maid for her first two years until she could afford the cheaper rate in her sorority. She graduated in 1938 as one of the few women with a degree in marketing and business.

After being offered a job as an elevator operator at a grand department store for $5 a week, she finally landed a job as a clerk with PA Department of Public Instruction in Harrisburg, PA. She and a girlfriend found an apartment, and they started to work.

CHAPTER 2

Courtship and Marriage

(SEPTEMBER 1939—JULY 1940)

WHEN OUR PARENTS MET AT THE PA DEPARTMENT OF PUBLIC Instruction in the fall of 1938, they were assigned a major task to work together: the writing of police training manuals to improve the quality of law enforcement in PA.

It was not love at first sight. Later letters suggest that Mom initially put up a cold, professional front between herself and Dad. Eventually, they began to spend time together, walking along the Susquehanna River and going to concerts during the summer of 1939.

Mom realized that Dad worked at a butcher shop on Saturday to pay his rent, but had no money for meals. She and her roommate began to cook dinner for the three of them during that summer, and it became clear that their romance was becoming serious. They made a decision to spend Christmas of 1939 with their own families in Pennsylvania and Connecticut.

Their relationship was becoming closer just as the events were overtaking Europe in the fall/winter of 1939. The first letter between them, which is saved, is one from Dad to Mom on Christmas night in 1939. This described a blissful peaceful scene of an American family at Christmas with no fears or anxieties of the hostilities in Europe, which were beginning to creep across the Atlantic. It was a point in time that stood still with an unconscious belief that their love could conquer all.

As the year turned to 1940, our parents continued falling in love and contemplating marriage. As the war worsened in Europe, it was on everyone's mind. Their parents tried to dissuade them from marrying, given the uncertainty as the Germans plowed through France, Belgium, and the Netherlands and reached the English Channel. By May 1940, the Germans were at the English Channel, and fear was gripping the United States. Dad's letters from May and early June described this palpable fear overcoming the United States, and my parents questioned whether they should get married.

At this very time, in the letters, there was the first mention that Mom was sick. It turned out that she had chronic anemia; it also impacted her liver. We were never aware of this problem as children, but throughout the first five years of their marriage, there was constant reference to her being "sick." This raised yet another concern about getting married, as she had to have various injections to improve her blood count.

As June began to turn to July, they make the decision to get married as the details were worked out. Their anxiety about the potential of a coming war only added to the stress.

The conflict of Americans about what to do was palpable in the next two letters as the opposing viewpoints of Lindbergh (the isolationists) and Roosevelt (Britain's supporters) flooded their lives. Meanwhile, they continued to live apart in Reading and Harrisburg, PA, only getting together on the weekends.

Dad's pondering of what this meant for his life and the wider world could not stifle his desire and need to be with Mom, as expressed in a letter days later. As he looked toward their lives together, its hope overcame the fear of the coming war.

Three weeks later, on July 12, 1940, Mom and Dad were married at the parsonage of the First Methodist Church in East McKeesport, PA—her hometown. Although our father's family in New London wanted to come to the wedding, they did not have the funds to travel by train or the money to buy gasoline for such a long auto trip. So, it was a simple affair with only our mother's immediate family attending, with a small reception for a few family friends. The groom arrived the night before the wedding, and the couple left the morning after. It is clear that both families had some resistance to the marriage, mostly related to the impending war.

Throughout their courtship, their jobs at the Department of Public Instruction at the State Capitol in Harrisburg, PA, and the Economy League in Reading kept them separated through the week, with quick moments of living together on the weekends.

Their wedding day did not end that separation. Given the end of the Depression and their poor-paying public service jobs, they could not find a place to live together until October 1, 1940, not the way they had imagined when starting their married life together.

LETTERS: DECEMBER 1939–SEPTEMBER 1940

‹············•············•

World War II Begins:[1]

September 1, 1939: Germany and Russia attacked Poland. England and France declared war on Germany.

After the collapse of Poland, Denmark, and Norway, the war moved into the eight-month period of the "phony war," where German and Russian troops are gathering strength but take no offensive action.

Christmas 1939 falls right in the middle of the phony war.

•············•············•

1   The major events and battles of WWII will be interspersed among the letters to provide a
     timeline and context for the family's letters in each chapter and will be printed in bold ital-ics.

December 25, 1939, 8:15 pm
172 Willets Ave.
New London, CT

Jeanne, my Darling,

Christmas night - Beautiful, clear, crisp, cold - brilliant moonlight - and I am missing you like the Dickens! We "had the tree" at eleven this morning - then the folks came for dinner. We were ten - very gay and a delicious dinner it was - roast turkey and all the fix-ins. Fanny, the colored girl who has been in faithful service two days a week for thirty years, came to cook the buzzard and did herself proud. None can cook a turkey like Fanny.

Byron and Arlene and Jack came; Mom and Dad and we three boys Herb, Ned and me, and of course, Dad's sister Aunty La and Grandpa Lonnie made the ten. . . .

After dinner, we got Lonnie started on some of his yarns. They are swell. I do hope you get to see and hear him soon. He is an old gaffer, now, and sentimental as old ones are. When he told the story of the submarine, Deutschland, that sank one of his tugs with all on board in 1916, his voice broke and quavered and tears streamed down his cheeks. The tears came again, when he told of going out to rescue the City of Columbus, in a bitter winter's gale off Vineyard Haven back in 1881. The passengers had had to climb up in the rigging in their night clothes to escape drowning and they had frozen and gone to their doom leaving the frozen dresses, rigidly arrested up in the rigging like ghosts! And now, 58 years afterward, the memories visibly moved the old man.

More of his yarns were funny. Like the time he took his exam for his master divers' license—he had one as an engineer and thus was only the second person in the US to have both an engineer's and master divers' license. He was proud as a peacock until he found that the first person honored was a woman who ran a barge on the Erie Canal!

So, the day has gone. Some of us went down to see Cousin Alma at the hospital. She had a splendid day, lovely food, and much rest. She and the new baby are right well. She apparently had a rather unpleasant siege, 14 hours on the delivery table! But all is well now, and she was gay and happy and quite strong tonight.

Now I am sitting quietly with Mom and Dad listening to the Firestone concert on the radio and writing to my love. Later, Ned, Jack, Eddie, and I are going to get together for a gab.

And so, another Christmas passes into oblivion. The old folks get older, the young ones old, and new ones come. I hope this Christmas shall be the last one we are not together. And so, my Duchess, as this Christmas night that finds us 500 miles apart, draws to a close, I salute you across the tides and wave a quiet tender kiss to the westward knowing it will find you tomorrow.

Good night now, my sweetest sweet. All my love, Donald.

◆ ⋯⋯⋯⋯ ◆ ⋯⋯⋯⋯ ◆

At the beginning of May 1940, the Germans are on the move with the Blitzkrieg, France, and the low countries of Belgium and the Netherlands are overrun

| WILLIAM ALONZO FONES, | RACE ROCK LIGHT – |
| DAD'S GRANDFATHER | BUILT BY WAF |

May 20, 1940
Pennsylvania Economy League
Reading, PA

My beloved Darling,

A busy day, poring over expenditure figures of the County. Then went to the movies to see "Waterloo Bridge"—so very sad and moving. Fills me with so much more love for you—even more than before.

I have never really begun to make love to you—I mean in the day-to-day sense—not our special meaning for the words. I mean the lovemaking that's done in the noon-day sun, on the street. How grand that I shall be seeing you again in less than 24 hours!

I am so full-up to here—of the War. I try to stifle it, put it out of my ken, forget it—see it in its distant perspective. But it smashes down my barriers and creeps between us. It must never creep between us. No matter what happens. If ever it should ensnarl our lives, we must surround it—face it—go through with it—get it done with and hope and pray that après le guerre fin we can find the fruition and the sublimation of our dreams.

That is why I want so much to get our life together started, established, and under way. So that no catastrophe or war can shake the foundation of our happiness of our life together.

Goodnight now, my Sweet. You must be careful, rest, and be strong so that every day you are away will help you to get well so that we can marry soon. Love, Don

◆ · · · · · · · · · · · ◆ · · · · · · · · · · · ◆

May 25, 1940

Darling -

In this topsy-turvy world such horrible things can happen in the twitch of an eye. There must be an unshatterable bond between us to keep us together, even though we must be apart because of our jobs. The calm, complacent life in which we had our childhood and our bringing up is no more. It is dead as a dodo and we live in a world of movement—swiftly changing scenes and dynamic action. . . . We yearn for a more rational, calm contemplative peace, but the world is as we find it and we must adjust to overcome it. See you at 7:43 on Tuesday at the Reading Station. I love you, always and forever. Don

◆ · · · · · · · · · · · ◆ · · · · · · · · · · · ◆

Sunday, June 16th, 1940 - 4 pm
Reading PA

Darling Sweet and Precious,
All rolled into one. What an empty weekend this has been.

. . .

*Mentally, I am nervous as a cat—ill-at-ease at not hav-
ing you with me. But I promised I would not carry on this
way. Saturday, we laid abed till 9—had our breakfast at home!
And wandered to town about noon. We found a State Moose
Convention in full celebration with a parade and all.*

*After dinner, we read and I began writing to you until Mr.
Lindbergh and the Little Giant (Arthur James, Republican gov-
ernor of PA) began to speak. Both worry me. Lindbergh because
of the truth and the cold analysis of his speech and his failure
to see the essentials of the war involved. James because of the
fact that one so stupid and so given to running off at the mouth
is in a high place and is seriously being considered by some for
higher office (Republican candidate for Vice-President). Both
are leaders in the America First—an isolationist party whose
basic premise is to avoid all contact with England to stay out of
the war.*

*Thus, reading myself to sleep, missing you like a jump-
ing toothache—lost, alone, afraid, uncomfortable, aimless, frus-
trated, unadjusted, out-of-sorts, and scared of what may come.*

◆ ⋯⋯⋯ ◆ ⋯⋯⋯ ◆

**June 22, 1940, the French surrender to the Germans and France is divided
into Vichy France (governed by Nazi collaborators) and Occupied France,
where the Germans are directly in control.**

◆ ⋯⋯⋯ ◆ ⋯⋯⋯ ◆

June 23, 1940 8:30 pm
Reading, PA

My darling,

. . Now it is a rainy summer night—a sad, breathless kind of night—quite in tune with the depressing and sad news from beyond the seas. I have noticed a strange tenseness both in Harrisburg and Reading yesterday and today.

Men's minds are not on their work. They are wondering: What will happen now? Does this mean we are closer or farther away? Isn't there some way out short of war? Must we go through this performance all over again? (Remembering WWI).

They, the men, don't say very much; that is the sound, sensible ones. In fact, they say nothing except to ask for the latest news. But their minds are not riveted on the job at hand as it usually is.

They are like I was last August and September (when the Germans and the Russians attacked Poland on September 1, 1939, beginning WWII). They cannot concentrate.

Even then it would have been too late for us to have done anything about it. It is a profound limitation to democracy that it cannot live in the same world with a form of government whose basic premise is force and arms. Thus, this time, we must not only destroy the disciples of force but destroy force, itself as a medium of national conduct.

George Townsend is indeed right in his belief in the futility of war—but unfortunately, his reliance on pacifism, letting the Axis beat the Allies over the head until the Fascists get tired, is too much to expect.

In the long, long run, it will probably be the better way, but I believe we can do away with war in the next 100 years. I wonder if I am an idealist. It will be interesting to see if any of the effects of the war resisters activity in the past few months will make a difference in this world conflagration.

June 25, 1940

Reading, PA

Dearest Beloved,

 Have you seen "Our Town?" Have I ever talked with you about it? Saw the play in Philly Thanksgiving of '38. I've just seen the movie and it's even better. I hope you see it and I hope you like it.

 To see the kids over their ice cream sodas is like falling in love with you all over again! It has a moral, of course—that is—it lights up the common-place, homely, routine act of every-day life and makes them stand out as stunning as stars. It makes plain living together a thrilling adventure. It makes such a simple quiet, unassuming, intimate little affair—yet as dignified and reverent a thing. I want you to see it and during the falling in love and wedding sequence, you must think of me as I was thinking of you; but your hand wasn't in mine and I missed you.

 I think I can be "altar and halter" broken after seeing that.

 I am sure worried about it, though. Scared nigh half to death, sometimes, it seems. You must be very gentle with me.

 Yours forever and ever, Don.

September 1940: The Germans begin their Blitz of the Brits by starting unceasing night bombing of London and other major cities. Many children are moved to the countryside with other families for safety. London becomes a shell of its former self and the Brits wait anxiously.

CHAPTER 3

First Two Years of Marriage

(JULY 1940—MAY 1942)

THROUGH FRIENDS, MOM AND DAD FOUND AN IDYLLIC IF spartan place to begin their married life. They were introduced to George Moore, a Reading banker, who had a farm estate, west of Reading in Wernersville, PA. Above his three-car garage was an apartment with a coal fired stove and no appliances for $35 per month, which pushed their budget to a busting point. An easy commute to Reading but over an hour to Harrisburg on bus and train.

Within weeks, good fortune fell into their laps. A friend of a friend was a state policeman who commuted daily from Wernersville to Harrisburg, so Mom had a ride to work. This was the magical moment that really started their married life together.

Although no letters survived from these first two years of their married life as they were seldom apart, we were told funny and poignant stories of their time on this farm. In addition, a 1945 letter that Mom wrote Dad while overseas, which described her memories of the "farm", concludes this chapter.

They began to create the kind of life they hoped to have for many decades to come. A big, lovable German Shepherd named Kurt wandered into their lives. There were some wonderful descriptions of Kurt. If one of them had to stay at their public service jobs late into their evening, Kurt would wander around their bed and hop in when it was clear that Mom or Dad would not be home. Or the time, our Uncle Bill who served on the European front came to visit and fell in love with Kurt. When they took Bill to the train and Kurt was left at home pining his loss, the big doggie took out his revenge by jumping on the kitchen table, eating the remainder of the Sunday roast beef. Kurt continued to play a role throughout their lives. Although he passed away sometime after the end of the war, Mom shared stories of Kurt even as her short-term memory faded into the 1990s.

UNCLE BILL WITH THE FAMILY DOG, KURT IN THE SNOW IN
WERNERSVILLE, PA

Their first two years of marriage were described by Mom and Dad in war time letters as both "wonderful and challenging." Mom continued to be weak and sickened from her "liver ailment." She quit her job due to her long commute, could not find a new one in Reading, and her inaction led to some significant depression. In other letters from the war, they also mentioned how their love life suffered during these first years. However, they both agreed that through these challenges, they found a way to talk through issues that demonstrated "respect, kindness, and affection for each other."

Meanwhile, the world was marching toward total madness. The events below were happening during the first two years of their marriage, and one can only wonder how these upsetting developments also impacted the marriage of two self-described "jittery, anxious" newlyweds. Pearl Harbor and America's entry into the war abruptly ended their calm, peaceful life on the farm.

◆ ·············· ◆ ·············· ◆

September 27, 1940: Germany, Italy, and Japan sign their Axis Pact, and the authoritarian and violent leaders combine into a formidable opponent.

March 11, 1941: Britain and the United States sign their Lend–Lease Agreement, so the Brits can keep their Navy and Air Force up to strength and supplied. The world holds their breath with the anticipation of the Germans actually crossing the Channel to conquer the British Isles. But the amphibious attack never materializes, and during spring/summer of 1941, the nightly raids of the English Royal Air Force with help from the Americans win the Battle of Britain.

June 22, 1941: Hitler makes the fateful decision to break Germany's non-aggression pact with Russia and begins to attack Russia, opening up a two-front war, which many historians claim foretells the Germans' ultimate defeat. But for most of 1941, the British are pushed to the limit.

December 7, 1941: Japan makes their surprise attack on Pearl Harbor in the Hawaiian Islands. Over 3,000 American lives are lost, and one-third of the Pacific fleet is destroyed. Simultaneously, Japan attacks numerous island chains in the Pacific as they move south and west toward Singapore,

Dutch New Guinea, and other British colonies. America declares war on Japan and Germany.

◆ ⋯⋯⋯⋯ ◆ ⋯⋯⋯⋯ ◆

In spite of these horrendous events, Mom and Dad had warm memories of their first two years of marriage. These memories are reflected in this letter from Mom to Dad after she revisits Wernersville with her mother in September 1945, driving back from New London to Pittsburgh.

◆ ⋯⋯⋯⋯ ◆ ⋯⋯⋯⋯ ◆

September 6, 1945

Poppa,

. . . Things have changed in Reading and Wernersville, but I am not sorry I went. It brought you so close to me —it was still the same lovely little house to me where we lived and loved—where we shared so many beautiful things—delightful memories—our pretty garden where we worked so hard—the Poppa making the speeches to the gobble-gobbles—the apple pies we made from the apples in the orchard— our first Christmas tree—the big doggie (Kurt) coming to live with us—the pear tree with first snowfall—the baby lambs and Cheerio—the pheasants down by the brook—the chestnut tree—the Poppa pushing the wheel barrow with the ashes—the little pussycat—the walks in the backfields—the moonlit nights we laid on the grass, watching the cars go by on the main road. Most of all, I remembered the love and pretty living in the little house with you —the joys and unhappiness we shared those first two years. So, I am not unhappy that I stopped by and you must not be unhappy when you read this. . . . The Punkin

CHAPTER 4

Training in Miami Beach: Dad goes to Reserve Officer Candidate School for the Army Air Corps

(MAY 15—JULY 15, 1942)

HOTEL RENDALE – DAD'S HOME FOR OFFICER CANDIDATE'S SCHOOL

OUR PARENTS' IDYLLIC LIFE IN THE PENNSYLVANIA COUNTRY-side came crashing down with the attack on Pearl Harbor. American men were confronted with tough decisions. Did they join up or did they wait to be drafted? Many college-educated men like Dad contemplated these decisions. Should they apply to be an officer or go in as an enlisted man? Dad applied to be an officer in either the Army Air Corps or the Navy. The Army Air Corps accepted him first and he went to Reserve OCS in Miami Beach, FL, on May 15, 1942, for a two-month training course focusing on administration and supervision. He was one of the older recruits at the age of 35 years.

Dad was in the third class of Reserve OCS. It was long hours of study and exams as well as physically hard work. He would graduate in mid-July 1942. Not knowing where he would be assigned, he invited Mom to the graduation, so he could see her briefly before he left Miami Beach for his first posting.

As Dad finished up his two-month training in Miami Beach and looked forward to Mom coming south for his graduation, the reality of a war-time marriage became clearer. Officers in training with the rank of first lieutenant made very little money. More surprising, they had to pay for their food, their uniforms, and their lodging out of their salary. Their wives were left at home with or without kids to provide for. Mom luckily had a job, but she had pay for all her expenses rather than sharing them with Dad. In addition, when Dad had gone back to graduate school at Penn, he was forced to take out loans from 10–12 relatives or friends. He had promised to pay them back and most of their friends and relatives were struggling to meet their own budgets.

Although Dad had been trained to work in the Inspector General's office to make sure all facilities, procedures, and processes were up to snuff and as safe as possible, there were still many uncertainties and fears. Where would they go? Could Mom go with him? When would he go overseas? Where? These financial pressures of moving and their fears of what was next, flood their letters.

LETTERS AND TIMELINE

◆ ⋯⋯⋯⋯ ◆ ⋯⋯⋯⋯ ◆

May-July 1942

May 6, 1942: The United States surrenders the Philippine Islands, a US Territory to Japan

◆ ⋯⋯⋯⋯ ◆ ⋯⋯⋯⋯ ◆

ON JUNE 6, 1942, THE ALLIES WIN THEIR FIRST MAJOR NAVAL victory in the Pacific, beating the Japanese at the Battle of Midway. This is the event that begins to turn the tide in the Pacific, but the officers in training know that this recovery of islands and colonies all across Asia and the Pacific will take years to accomplish.

◆ ⋯⋯⋯⋯ ◆ ⋯⋯⋯⋯ ◆

June 21, 1942
Miami Beach, FL

My lovely Punkin,

Now it's bedtime and I haven't talked with you today. How you've been and what are all the little things—mysteries, vague and shadowy, like in a dream?

Today was one of those blank days; I suppose they are necessary when we work at this 14-hour per day pace, but I'd rather work harder, it seems, and get this temporary business over with—so I can get started with our real job and the Punkin is with me.

But I must admit the first three weeks have gone like lightning when I think back at what's been accomplished. It seems puerile and feckless for me to keep repeating how much I love you; how much I miss you—but when I'm not thinking Army-Air Force, that's all I can think of.

You have been a wonderful wife. You have put up with so much and have been a good soldier. Two long years we have been married, and it seems as though we've hardly started.

We may have to celebrate our anniversary a day or two early. If they do as they did with the class 1942 B, we'll leave on a special train on Saturday at 9 pm (confidential). So, Sunday, the 12th, we'll be going in different directions. But we will join hands soon—we must.

You are one, the only one for me. You will be proud of Papa—belly in—shoulders straight—tanned all over—just like Tarzan! We will make such wonderful love! Hurry! I love you like sixty! Poppa

◆┄┄┄┄┄◆┄┄┄┄┄◆

Friday, June 26, 1942
Miami Beach, FL

You poor, precious darling, worrying yourself sick about money and old Uncle Sam is owing us so much. Sending a check for $60. This will get you down (to Miami Beach), and then we can see where we stand and what we must do. Somehow, I got the impression you were out of the woods—but I've had so many things to absorb and digest that I didn't realize how short you've been. I still have 20 more to last until July 2 or 3 when we are supposed to be paid, and I don't need any down here except for laundry and cigarettes and pocket money. So, if you need more before you leave, let me know.

Now then, my brave old hero, you must your buckle up, put up the chin and face the fact that the situation is rapidly getting to a very serious stage—I MEAN THE WAR.

I am surer, more than ever at least one half of our group (Class 1942 C) will be in some kind of field services by October! Perhaps by Labor Day! That means we must make every minute between now and then count like sixty.

And if you can possibly get here sooner than July 3rd, i.e., Wednesday, Thursday, or even Tuesday, you must try to get reservations shoved ahead and get down here, pronto. I won't know anything anymore definite until the very last minute and even then, I'll not know when you can join me. But at least we'll have snatches of a few days together.

I'll be busy as the devil with courses right up to Wednesday of the last week. Some of us have been ordered to take a special advanced course in Administration for two hours a day, beginning on Monday. So, it looks like I'm down for an administrative job—somewhere—but that doesn't mean "desk work" only, and it doesn't mean "zone of the interior" (U.S.) only.

Administrative, supply, and mess officers—all of which are the main products of this school—are being assigned to task forces and being moved to embarkation points every day. Some are even being taken out of our group only 2/3 of the way through the program and they disappear—leaving all manner of rumors behind. Stories coming back about assignments of Classes A & B graduates, who have moved out since I landed here, are incredible. The need for officers is apparently frightening!!! Needless to say, this is not to be mentioned. I could be thrown out for telling you. Love, Poppa

CHAPTER 5

Dad's First Posting in Enid, OK

DON AT DESK

FIRST LIEUTENANT DONALD DUNN ASSIGNED TO BE ASSIS-
tant Inspection Officer, Enid Army Air School (July 15–December 15, 1942)

As our parents part at the railroad station in Jacksonville, FL, after his graduation from OCS, he slipped her the following note:

....

July 11, 1942
1:00 pm

Jeanne,

Here is a copy of our orders sending me to Enid, OK. Do not let anyone else have it. (The word restricted means, for the information of military personnel only.) But you can show it to prove the necessity for getting yourself to Enid; larger gasoline stations will ordinarily honor it for unlimited gasoline purchases on route to Enid—it also may help getting recapped tires to replace the worn-out tires on the 38 Pontiac. Love, D

....

This began another four-month separation of our parents following the two-month hiatus while he was in OCS; six months apart was not easy in their second year of marriage. This separation and their workloads began to put major stress on our parents' relationship. There were two or three letters a week as Dad tried to persuade Mom to pack up their furniture and belongings and ship it out to Enid and come herself. Although Dad was underwhelmed with the environment of Enid, OK—102 degrees, dusty, dry, and few trees—he tried to sell her on the idea of renting or possibly buying a new home, one of 20 set on an abandoned field from Oklahoma's dust bowl days. He shared the progress on the house every few days. There were incessant discussions about how to get their belongings out there and how Mom would drive their bald-tired old Pontiac halfway across the country by herself.

Traveling by car for any distance for four years of war had become difficult. Gasoline was severely rationed and depending on your classification, you might not be able to get gas. In addition, getting new tires was almost impossible. Synthetic rubber had not been invented and all rubber planta-tions of the SW Pacific and Asia were now under Japanese control.

As July and August flew by, Mom was given a promotion, which entailed working seven days per week. The non-profit needed her adminis-trative skills as the men were being drafted or joining up. If she quit her job, they realized that Dad's earnings of $287 per month had to support both of them since it was not clear what kind of job she could get in Enid, especially not knowing how long Dad would be stationed there. Dad understood her reluctance and supported her decision not to quit her job, but his desire and need for her companionship was intense.

In spite of the long work hours Mom experienced, she realized she liked the new and difficult work, a CFO for the non-profit. One letter demon-strated how she was conflicted about leaving Reading for Enid.

As August moved into September, Dad and Mom were still struggling under the stress. Dad was given a second job beyond his inspection duties for the base. He was made the adjutant commander of a squadron for 200 cadet pilots. He was in charge of all their needs: medical, psychological, dis-ciplinary, and organization of their training, both in-flight and classroom. He was working seven days a week. Mom's health was worsening and still she was also working seven days per week. Her worsening chronic liver condition with a low red blood count—anemia was being exacerbated by overwork and stress.

Communication continued to be difficult through September and October 1942 as Mom's medical condition got worse. She put their belong-ings in storage as their lease ended and drove to East McKeesport with her mother who had helped her pack up the little house.

Having arrived home in East McKeesport, one of her first stops was at her regular doctor who warned her of the consequences of not taking care of herself.

Dad's own mother got a letter from Mom who shared her plight with her mother-in-law. Grandma Leo sent her son a couple of letters, trying to explain why Mom was resisting the idea of moving to Enid and encouraging him to take some leave and go to Pittsburgh to see her. She encouraged him to go, so he would get an idea about how sick Mom was and, more importantly, communicate with Mom more directly and express his love for her.

Dad got a five-day leave to go see Mom in Pittsburgh, as his mother had suggested. He hitchhiked via Army Air Corps planes. He hoped Mom would let him drive them both back to Enid, but Mom's talks with her doctor had convinced her she could not make a 40-hour non-stop trip, given her illness. Their time together seemed to rekindle their relationship. Dad understood that Mom needed complete rest for six weeks to two months while she was under the care of her doctor. Disappointed but feeling better about their relationship, he flew back to Enid.

LETTERS AND TIMELINE (JULY 20–DECEMBER 15, 1942)

July 28, 1942
Enid, OK

My Sweetest Punkin,

Went to movies last night. The picture was very lovely— more love story, in fact, than baseball. And tonight, I love you more and more. You are to me what Mrs. Lou (Gehrig) was to Lou Gehrig—and I hope you get to see the picture, so you'll know what I mean. You must hurry! Every minute you are away from me is a minute taken from the precious interval we have before the real and awful separation comes—which I dare not contemplate (going overseas). That interval of bliss we'll have together may be six months or a year; it may be six days—no one can tell. All the forces in this horrid war can impinge upon the turn of luck with the fateful day.

This, then, is argument to prevail against all other (to come to Enid). But do not worry, my little one. Be assured and wise in your decisions, with full faith and knowledge that I love you dearly, that I'll always love you so, that I shall never be anything but faithful and true too. Today, we were issued gas masks for our maneuvers tomorrow. Tomorrow, we get issued rifles and packs.

So, it goes big shots and little ones—all working like horses, trying to make every precious minute here count for its utmost.

I love my Punkin! Poppa

August 15, 1942
Reading, PA

Dear Poppa,

I have been thinking of how soon I can be with you and be able to stay by your side as long as it is possible. That is the only important thing for me to do—it would not be fun doing it without you, my dearest one. But it does makes me feel good after struggling hard to achieve some recognition professionally—to know that things are shaping up here now (my new job). But if I must decide what to do, I want to be with you, helping you, and being where you want me.

Your Punkin, Jeanne

August 22, 1942
The little house

My dearest sweetheart,

You are so wonderful, writing so many lovely letters and getting so few from me. I try so hard to be able to get a few words off to you, but these past two days have been such hectic ones at work that I am exhausted when I get home. The heat has been terrific, especially at work, and I am all worn out. If mother wasn't here, I don't know what I'd do. My mom has been a tremendous help, getting up in the morning, getting me breakfast, packing my lunch—then having dinner ready for me in the evening.

Your Punkin

•••••••••••••••━━━••••••••••••••

September 1, 1942
Enid Army Air Base

My wonderful Punkin,

Now today comes word that you are up to your neck in a new job! So, it goes. You can't very well walk out on Mr. Werner because he was nice to us when you needed a job, and apparently, he needs you badly right at this point. But I need you, too, my Punkin—and just as soon as you can, you must tell them that your "Lootenant" needs you to come to him and you must leave. The work should be well enough along, so you can leave by October 1 for sure, luckily before maybe. I shall have more to say about the progress of the house and moving in in our call on Sunday.

Forever yours, Poppa

•••••••••••••••━━━••••••••••••••

September 7, 1942
Enid Army Air Base

Dear Punkin,

I tried to write you after I finished Dr. Sweeney's letter (his thesis advisor and my godfather), but all I could turn out was a nasty fulmination, ill-tempered, and unworthy of my lovely one.

So now I have a call in for you, because I must hear your voice. It's been six weeks since I left you in JAX and it's too long— and at least another four weeks and maybe more to go.

What I was trying to say this afternoon was all snarled up. I'm afraid you are getting tired out and then you'll be mad with me, like you were last winter when you weren't well. And we mustn't let that happen again.

Don't worry, my Punkin. Don't worry about the new house. Don't worry about the moving. If you think we shouldn't move the furniture out, let's put it in storage. We can take a furnished place as soon as we can get it. This is why I called you on Sunday.

Love, Poppa

◆••••••••••◆••••••••••◆

This letter was found unopened in its envelope in Mom's papers but torn in half.

September 16, 1942: War news continues to improve in the Pacific. Allied navy and army air forces score a huge victory at Guadalcanal, which costs many thousands of lives but offers hope that the Philippine Islands will be taken back.

◆••••••••••◆••••••••••◆

September 15, 1942
East McKeesport, PA

Dearest Don,

The last two times I have been at the doctor's, I have not reacted any too well to the injections. I presume it was a nervous reaction, for he did not do so well in putting in the needle, and then I was so terribly upset and nervous—with all the work that is piled up on me and all this trouble with the moving.

I am sorry if I seemed nasty and disgruntled when I talked with you on the phone Sunday. It seemed like everything was piling up on me and then to get your letter about those bank notes I had forgotten was the last straw. My head has been so full of thoughts—and just as things begin to look a little clearer, something else pops up and my head feels as though it is going into little pieces. The Momma certainly is going to pieces fast.

I am sorry I cannot write any love tonight. I am utterly devoid of love for anything or anyone, even you. That is nasty, isn't it, but I cannot express love, feeling the way I do.

Your Punkin, Jeanne

◆ ⋯⋯⋯⋯ ◆ ⋯⋯⋯⋯ ◆

September 25, 1942
East McKeesport, PA

Dearest Don,

I had just given up hope of hearing from you, but from your letter I can see you must be very, very busy. And I have been too. The days go by so fast, and it seems I don't get much accomplished. Too many worries, I presume, and I can't concentrate on the immediate job of getting packed.

Your telegram came on Sunday afternoon shortly after I had come home from work, and frankly, I was very much upset about it. Perhaps it was because I was exhausted from working and very much upset that the car went flooey. It made me quite angry—everyone, even you, do not seem to consider me at all. It seems like I am a puppet on a string and every time the string is pulled, I am supposed to jump. Well, I am through jumping around and am going to do things the way I want to. You are probably angry now, but I need to get it off my chest. You have no conception of what I have been going through this last month, trying to organize things, having one setback after another, financial worries by the hundred and working like a dog to keep things going. I am tired and sick, and I admit it but only because I've had to carry the load myself and have come to the point where I am utterly exhausted.

I finish work on September 26 and the movers are coming on Tuesday, September 29. From that time on, it's up to you, Don, to assume some of the responsibilities and take care of me. I am quitting my job much against my better judgement, for I know exactly what happened before when I did that.

And this much I want understood. I do expect you to find some time between now and the time I get to Enid to get a place for us to live. I know you are going to be very much upset when you get this letter, but I am telling you I am at the breaking point, both physically and mentally, and either you've got to start being my husband and accepting the responsibilities as such, or else we had better call it quits. You have always come first with me in every respect, but I think if you will consider everything very closely, I have not always come first in your heart.

Good night now—down deep, I guess I really love you very much, but sometimes love can turn into indifference—and that is something which I cannot tolerate.

Yours, Punkin

October 2, 1942
East McKeesport, PA

Dear Don,

Went down to see doc this evening. He gave me particular hell for going to such a horse doctor in Reading and paying him money for treatments I got. So, beginning Monday, I am going into him each day to get my liver injections and some other injections. When I am ready to leave, he is to give me the names of the medicines and insists that when I get to Enid you make arrangements at the Post for me to get the same injections. What he will give me should carry me until I get to Enid, but he says I must get the injections very soon after I arrive, or little Jeannie is going to go poof. The old doc really gave me hell. Told me he was sick and tired of my not taking care of myself.

I am so glad you were able to find an apartment for us. I am sorry that the little house did not work out, but I think that is for the best.

My last letter hurt you, I know. I am sorry if it did, but when the Momma is sick, she does not care who she hurts. This time I have really pushed myself to the falling place. I don't want to come out to you sick and tired and worn out, which I am now. So, you must have patience with me. . .

It would be wonderful if you were able to meet me part way so we can drive to Enid together. The thought of making the trip all by myself makes me shudder, yet I want to get going and keep on moving. The thing inside me that makes me want to go on and on until I am ready to drop just will not let up, and I am boiling inside to keep on going. I am so keyed up that sitting around and doing nothing at home here is already beginning to drive me crazy.

You certainly picked a hell of a woman for your wife, but that's what you get for letting yourself be roped in by a blonde.

Good night to my darling. I do love you, but I have been sidetracked by the world and its demands. I am sorry, but I have given my best. Surely, you can't ask for more.

Love, Punkin

October 5, 1942
Enid, OK

Darling,

Forgot to put a stamp on this letter, so it has been held up. I am leaving on a troop train. Will be back in 72 hours and hope to have five days' leave to drive you to Enid. Cannot tell where my cross-country "airplane hitchhike" will take me, but I should know by Friday. Will phone, so be ready for immediate departure.

My mother told me of Pop's death (his grandfather). So, I am phoning New London tonight. Completely impossible for me to travel to the funeral, given this trip. I shall return on Thursday, and I will phone and state when and where to meet me!

Love, D.

My mind is a complete fuzz. Don

October 8, 1942
East McKeesport, PA

Dearest Sweetheart,

I know that you are still disappointed that we could not ride back to Enid together, driving straight through. I simply must get enough of those injections, dear, to carry me until I get to OK. You must get it in your head, darling, that I am sick. I am sick and down to rock bottom this time. As Doc put it today, "If you want to commit suicide, go ahead and get it over with, but don't prolong it the way you are doing." Sometimes, I get so angry with you, I don't want it to be that way; it only builds up a wall between us and if we are not careful, someday, we won't be able to break down the wall. . .

Goodnight, sweetheart. How I wish you were here beside me, so I could touch your hand, and say, "Sweetheart, wake up, put your arms around me. I am so afraid."

The Punkin

◆·············◆·············◆

October 15, 1942
New London, CT

Dearest Donald

From the bottom of my heart, I'm sorry for you and Jeanne. I know how much you want her with you. I know how much she wants to be with you. Such a discouraging letter from her the other day. Of course, she has had too much to do. But there was no way out of it. I know what a tough job she had because I have had a tough job—a man's job, too. Although I'm much older, I believe I'm much stronger. I think a little quick rest will get her started on the road to recovery. If she just can relax and rest. She said you hoped to get into Ohio to meet her. Can't you possibly hop a plane to Pittsburgh and spend a few hours with her even if she isn't able to accompany you back? It will do you both good and you can see for yourself just how ill she is, and to have you visit her will make her want to get on her feet to get out there with you. It would seem that you might have a few days granted to you to visit her since she is ill. All my love to both of you, Mom

CHAPTER 5

Loss and Financial Hardship in Dad's Family: New London

(JULY 1942–DECEMBER 1942)

LEONORA (LEO) FONES DUNN & HERBERT LUTHER DUNN

THIS CHAPTER SHARES A PICTURE OF WHAT MANY AMERICAN families were experiencing on the home front during this first year of the war. Although the war brought economic advantages to some families with increased job opportunities, those who were in the service and had elderly parents had many expenses beyond their means. Also, these opportunities were not initially equally divided among whites, blacks, Hispanics, and other ethnic groups across the country. Here is a picture of how Dad's family was faring in New London, CT.

Since she was 10 years old, Dad's mother, Leo, had lived at her father's home at 172 Willets Ave. This home now needed to be sold, given their diminishing income. Given her father's and husband's decline, Grandma Leo was responsible for emptying a 15-room house by herself to move into a smaller, rental home some blocks away. Both her boys (Dad and Ned) were in the service, and we heard of her struggles economically and emotionally in letters to Dad during the summer and fall of 1942.

There were similar economic struggles that existed with middle-class families across the country. Social Security was just starting and the letter that Dad had written the Social Security Office requesting benefits for his father was as detailed as applying for a mortgage application today. Even with that, neither he nor our grandmother qualified for benefits. This was a middle-class family that had dropped out of the middle class and was approaching poverty as their health failed and our grandfather could not work regularly. All the sons attempted to send their parents monthly checks, but it was just not enough to support a family of four: Pop (Lonnie), Leo, her husband Herb, and his maiden sister, Ella.

These letters also reflected how families communicated with each other in the 1930s and 1940s. In emergencies, they sent telegrams, and only occasionally, did they use the telephone. They mostly sent letters. A first-class letter was 1 cent, airmail 3 cents. A three-minute call could be 3 dollars. In most towns and small cities, there were two mail deliveries per day and two pick-ups.

The use of telegrams, even in the case of close family death, is illustrated below.

Dad's grandfather, William Alonzo Fones—Lonnie—died in early October 1942. His daughter, Dad's mother, sent Dad a telegram telling him of grandfather's death. But Dad, although he had grown up with Lonnie his entire life, could not leave his service duties to return for the funeral.

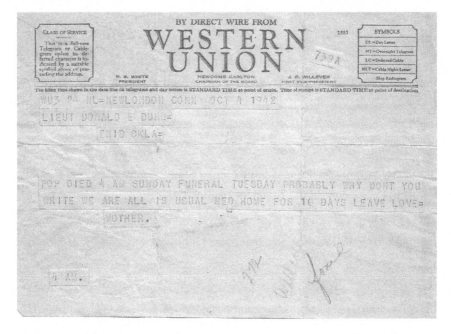

WILLIAM ALONZO FONES – DEATH TELEGRAM TO MY FATHER IN ENID, OK

LETTERS FROM OUR GRANDMOTHER LEO, DAD'S MOTHER, TO OUR DAD (JULY 1942–DECEMBER 1942)

July 14, 1942
New London, CT

Dearest Donald,

These hot days, and yesterday so muggy and rainy and today so hot again. It hasn't been so good for Dad. Saturday, after he came home from work at 3:30 p.m. and went to bed, he did not awaken until near 8 o'clock. And yesterday he spent all day resting and napping. Today, he came home at his usual time and has gone directly to bed. As yet would take nothing to eat. But I'll fix some hot milk for him to have in the night.

Pop is quite exhausted too. He doesn't sit up very much, only just long enough to eat his meals. Selling his home that he built in 1890 was quite a blow to him, and I have tried to make it as easy as possible. I don't know how I lived through it myself. I surely never put over such a program in my life. It really was a man's job anyway and I had to be the man.

Our bill at Gardiner's (the furniture movers) was $61.00. And as yet, I haven't paid Millie the egg man for his own trucking and help. Nor Mr. Ward for his extra hours. The loads and loads they brought down after working hours on Saturday afternoon. But we are all here and am I glad. I think I am the only one who is glad, but you know how long I've wanted a better house and now I have it.

I do wish I had one more bedroom. I have your studio couch in a little closet just as tight as it could be. Had the door taken off and I get in over the foot of the bed. But it's a very good place for me to sleep near Dad and Pop, who need help *throughout the night. Pop and Aunt Ella (her maiden sister-in-law who is 80) have the two really fine bedrooms.*

I am delighted that you spend time writing to me. And now that our rush is over, I will be more punctual about our letters. I hope you keep us informed about your whereabouts. We are anxious to know as much of your life as you can describe. Censoring of all mail from military bases and overseas is happening. Glad you are enjoying your training. It won't hurt you to lose a few pounds. I am sleepy. Will write to Jeanne tomorrow and will send you another letter later in the week. All our love to you. Dad absolutely loves your letters. Mom

•·············◆·············•

August 6, 1942
New London, CT

Dearest Donald,

Just a few minutes before the evening mail is collected to get a letter to you. I have neglected you, I know, and your nice notes came today. Many, many thanks for your attention. You can't realize what it means to both Dad and me.

Jeanne (Mom) also sent me such a lovely letter and those splendid snapshots! She promises me a few days before she goes to Enid, she will come to see us. I shall so want to have her; I am very, very glad she is going to be with you, and I hope you are to be permanently located. If you can't be any nearer than Oklahoma, I am very thankful it is no farther away.

Last week was so full. Dad was at home ill for the whole week. Just pure exhaustion. When he gets that tired out, then the old heart acts up and just has to lie in. The doc says there is no more to do than what he is doing and just rest in bed is the only help. Dad went back to work today. He is tired but not that exhausted.

Last Thursday at 5 a.m., the doorbell rang. I thought it might be your brother Ned and sure enough it was Ned on a 48-hour leave from Norfolk and the Coast Guard base. He left on the 11:30 p.m. train on Friday night. Brother Herb was here for a day with Abbie and Grace Elizabeth. Glad to see all hands-on deck except for Jeanne and you, but busy and tired when all left. Must run to the corner to meet the mailman. All our love to you, Mom and Dad

<hr />

October 15, 1942
New London, CT

Dear Don,

I am gradually getting rested—I was so tired because I did have a very hard two weeks. The funeral arrangements for Pop were all made by the Prentice Funeral Home.[2] And everyone said what a beautiful service it was. I did not have to think of one thing. All I will have to do is pay for the bill—$400. Pop's insurance of $3,000 paid one half by Merritt, Chapman Scott, the larger national marine salvage business that bought the family-owned company and the other half taken from the monthly check is made out to me.

So, $500 of that will clear up everything I owe. Then I have to try to limit our expenses. While Dad can still work, we will get on all right. Our income will take care of the rent here and other expenses. Yesterday was my day out. I went for the rent collections.[3] Cousin Alma invited me to her house for lunch.

---

2   Her dad who lived in their home, William Alonzo Fones—Lonnie—died at 86 on October 4, 1942.

3   The family must have had small properties around New London since the rents total only about $75 per month—she literally had to walk around New London once a month to collect the rent.

Do cheer up—things will straighten out for you like the crossword puzzle. Before you know it, all will be solved. At least Jeanne has given up the job and the furniture is stored. Get leave and go see her. Always our love to you.

Mom

————◆————

My Dad's brother, Ned, a 22-year-old Coast Guard seaman, also wrote to his brother, encouraging him to "think about others, including their parents," even if he was stressed with his work as a captain in the Army Air Force.

————◆————

October 1, 1942
New London, CT

Dear Buddie,

What in the hell is the matter with you? Don't they let you write letters in the Army Air Corps or did the censor destroy all your letters to Mom? You make me sore. Here she is, doing a valiant job holding the home front, and you don't even so much as send a wire on her birthday. Even I did more than that. Pop is very definitely on the downward path, requiring constant attention. Dad, thank the Lord, is well. Abbie and Herb are here adding to the confusion and I am home on 10 days' leave. Abbie pitches in and helps around and bolsters the morale; nevertheless, confusion reigns. And you definitely do not help by not writing. I try to write twice a week. How about it, let's get on the ball? Ned

————◆————

January 4, 1943: The allied forces recapture Dutch New Guinea.

CHAPTER 6

Two Years of Army Air Corps Living in a Pleasant Plains Community

(JANUARY 1943–DECEMBER 1944)

HOUSE UNDER TREES IN GARDEN CITY KANSAS

DAD WAS MADE A CAPTAIN IN DECEMBER 1943 AND WAS transferred to Garden City, Kansas, where Mom joined him after she had recovered from her liver ailment. The first indication that Mom has joined Dad in the western plains was a letter from Dad addressed to Mom at the Hotel Warren in Garden City, KS, postmarked January 8, 1943. He was in Sherman, TX, where he was involved in a training while Mom was looking for a place to live. The letter sounded like Mom was well, their relationship was good, and they had moved to Garden City.

Few letters were exchanged during 1943 and 1944 since they were lucky to be in one house in Garden City for almost exactly two years. The few letters that exist always were addressed to 912 1st Street, Garden City, KS. Mom had found them a wonderful place to live. The picture of the house above in 2019 reflects some renovation, but showed a large bungalow built in 1939 in a peaceful, quiet neighborhood where they were able to settle down for two lovely years.

The letters indicated that our parents shared a house with Maxine and Howard Blanchard. For much of the time, they shared the house with only Maxine because Howard was overseas with the Army Air Force. In addition, there were other names mentioned as living there, as people would come for two to four months and then get shipped out. Housing for married officers was difficult, as these small towns would balloon in population without any on-base housing for married officers.

However, the close relationships did endure. I have strong memories of seeing Christmas cards from the Blanchard's as a 10-year-old, who always inquired about my brother and me—as well as a loving letter from Maxine when Dad died in 1964. Other families come to mind: the Hollands, Zeitzes, and Dubois. Some remained Christmas card pals for the rest of their lives, while there were occasional visits if they happened to be in the Northeast.

Another wonderful memory was taking my brother Chris to Y camp and as mom was helping to unpack his footlocker, one of these old friends was unpacking their son's belongings across the cabin. A tearful, exuberant reunion occurred among two old friends who shared two years of their lives together in a dusty town in southern Kansas.

There seemed to be two kinds of letters between our parents in 1943 and 1944. During each of the years, it appeared that Mom would travel back to Pittsburgh, PA, and spent a month with her parents usually during spring. Dad would write to her there. He was lonely, but they had made friends, having lived in Garden City for close to two years. The only other time they would write to each other was when Dad was away at a month-long training for fiscal administration of large units of the Army Air Corps.

Mom, for the first time in her adult life, did not have a job, but when Dad was promoted to Captain and eventually Major, Mom became a mid-level officer's wife. Social life revolved around captains and majors, the mid-level officers at the Garden City Army Air Training base. Officers' wives tended to socialize in the same groups, whether it was at bridge parties, benefit social events or weekend evenings at the Officer's Club with dances and parties. The lieutenant colonels and colonels and their families seemed to congregate together as well. In smaller bases like Garden City, there was integration across all these groups, but there were strict social protocols that were followed depending on their rank. And, of course, the generals and their families were in a class of their own.

In one letter to Mom, Dad said the lead colonel's wife had asked for Mom to be in charge of the May officer's ball. Since our parents were going on leave during that time, he had to regrettably decline, but after checking with her, offered Mom's services for the July ball.

One other pattern of our parents' lives during 1943 and 1944 was getting a three-week leave each year during the late spring and early summer. Since Mom was often in Pittsburgh, she would meet Dad in New York and travel by train to Dad's family home in New London, CT, for about 10 days at the beach. Dad spoke movingly of wanting to spend time in New York in one letter to Mom.

These visits to New London were important for both Mom and Dad as well as his parents. A look from the future made the summer of 1944 visit even more poignant. The last picture ever taken of Grandpa Dunn and his two sons, Dad and Uncle Ned, is above. In less than a year, Dad was on his way to the Pacific, not to return until a few days before his dad died in the spring of 1946. His mom only lasted for three more years—Spring 1949.

LETTERS AND TIMELINE (JANUARY 1943–DECEMBER 1944)

January 8, 1943
Sherman, Texas

My dearly beloved,

I am missing the Punkin like 60 million. Have been fighting off a grippe cold ever since I left. But I guess we have to adjust to not knowing anything definitely until after it happens.

One thing I know definitely is that if ever the time comes that I have to leave the Punkin for real (going overseas), it will be hard, hard, harder than ever. Without the Punkin, I get lost. You act as a steadying influence—a balance wheel. Without you I worry—I am a "worry-wart." I worry about you—about the job—about the war—our folks, etc. With you, I eat, fall asleep, and grow fat, but maybe I won't be so bad. In fact, I can't with this new job because I'll have to work 20 hours a day or more. I don't know exactly when I will be back, maybe Sunday. I'll call you on Saturday to let you know.

Good luck with apartment hunting. Hope the basement apartment pans out alright. I love you like everything

Your Poppa

February 2, 1943: The German Army surrenders at Stalingrad

May 17, 1943
Garden City, KN

My most wonderful one,

Monday morning—much rested—a beautiful cool pink morning. Bad thunderstorm last night about 7 p.m. I guess I told you I flew the final report I had been working on to Dodge City, KN, to the Inspector General with Major Marr. Then, Thursday came the big let-down—put my feet up and loafed most of Thursday and Friday. Saturday, however, the holiday was over, and I was back in the old push again. Came home and fell asleep two nights in a row at 6 p.m. and slept through till the morning.

Art got back from his training, so the Dubois asked me to be on hand for dinner on Sunday at 5. Then Major and Mrs. Marr called me yesterday morning. So, I had fried chicken at 1 p.m. and fried pheasant at 5 p.m.

Love you, Don

OFFICERS AROUND CAPTAIN DONALD E. DUNN'S
DESK AT GARDEN CITY, KS BASE

July 10, 1943: The Allies invade Italy.

Two months later, in September 1943, Italy surrenders.

◆•••••••••••◆•••••••••••◆

April 24, 1944
Garden City, KN

My darling,

I wanna spend a day or two in NY on the way home from our leave this summer of 44. I want to hear music—rejuvenate my soul —with a ride on the Staten Island Ferry. I want to spend time in Central Park—go up on top of Radio City—go into St. Patrick's and walk on the Brooklyn Bridge. But mostly, all I want to do is have the effects of change set in before I get home or go off to the Pacific for god knows how long. Sweet. I'm tired—tired of routine, tired of Kansas, dust, rain, and mud. I need this day or so in between to make the vacation come to life. Can't wait. Don

◆•••••••••••◆•••••••••••◆

The Allies launch their land, sea, and air invasion of occupied France on D-Day—June 4, 1944

Just as all the Dunns, Leo and Herb, their children and spouses; Jeanne and Don; Herb and Abbie; and Maud and Ned are spending time on Ocean Beach in New London, CT.

◆•••••••••••◆•••••••••••◆

June 15, 1944
New London, CT

Dearest Donald,

This is the first possible moment I have had to write to you since you left a week ago last Wednesday. I really haven't come up for a breath until just today. Little Miss Grace Elizabeth is just awfully cute but believe me she gave Grandmama "a run for her money" alright. I never had to keep so busy in my life.

It was so good to see you and Jeanne and to see you both so well. We enjoyed every minute you were here, even the first half hour when you caught me getting ready to bathe and dress! The time was too short. When we think how many months had passed since we had seen you. Nevertheless, we were mighty glad you could make the trip. I hope the rest of your visit and return was as perfect. With a baby to take care of and Dad sick, it has been hard.

Love you.

Mom

HERBERT L. DUNN WITH HIS TWO SONS MAJOR DONALD DUNN
AND SAILOR NED DUNN AS THEY LEAVE FOR ACTIVE DUTY IN
THE SUMMER OF 1944.

***

June 22, 1944: The Soviets begin their offensive against the Germans.

August 15, 1944: The Allies begin to invade southern France. The Germans are being approached from the East, North, and South.

On October 23, 1944, the Americans win the sea Battle of Leyte Gulf.

***

ALL THIS GOOD WAR NEWS WAS ENCOURAGEMENT TO THE soldiers on the front as well as the soldiers back in the States. It appeared that the Allies were getting the upper hand in both Europe and in the Pacific. All were hoping that the war would be over in Europe in the next five to six months. But the soldiers who were slated to go the Pacific knew that this next part of the war might continue for years. In addition, the Allies suffered a major setback in late December 1944.

Just as it appears that the Allies are closing in on the Germans, Hitler orders one last-ditch stand in snowy mid-December 1944 near the German French border. The Battle of the Bulge, starting on December 16, 1944, takes thousands of American lives, and the area is not under control again until after the first of 1945.

CHAPTER 7

On the Move — Two Months in Waco, TX: Dad is promoted to major and reassigned to Waco, TX, Army Airfield (December 1944)

OUR PARENTS HAVE HAD THE GOOD FORTUNE TO BE IN Garden City for two years. His promotion indicated that things were about to change, and he was more than likely on his way to the Pacific.

Finally, on December 16, 1944, specific news of their departure from Garden City to Waco, TX, came from Mom's younger brother, Bill, who had been drafted at the age of 24 and was in a 16-week Basic Training program at Camp Hood, TX. News about the whereabouts of both our parents and Bill were described in his subsequent letters. He first wrote to his sister about his boot camp experience in the fall of 1944.

LETTERS (OCTOBER 1944–MARCH 1945)

October 7, 1944
Camp Hood, TX

Dear Jeanne,

I received your letter and the $10 yesterday. It sure came in handy. Last week, I think, was the hardest week we'll ever have. We were out till after 11 o'clock every night, and two of the days we only had C-field rations. They are pretty lousy, but when you work all day, you'll eat anything, I guess. If you can get any candy or cookies or care to bake a cake, I sure would appreciate it. Tell Don I said hello and congratulations on his appointment to Major. Hope to hear from you soon.

Bill.

December 16, 1944

Dear Jeanne,

I received your letter yesterday with the money, thanks a lot. Well, today they gave us two plans for taking leave after 16 weeks are up on January 17. We can leave earlier if we pay our own way or at government expense if we go on a troop train. Will you please find out about plane reservations or faster train reservations? Let me know as soon as possible about what you find out.

I hope that you and Don get located alright in Waco and have a nice trip down to Texas from Kansas.

Bill

January 10, 1945
Ft. Meade, MD

Dear Jeanne and Don,

Just a short note to let you know I am now at Fort Meade in Maryland. I pulled in on Tuesday morning at 9 a.m. We were given a complete physical, issued most of our new overseas equipment, and had our personal affairs taken care of. I don't believe we'll be here for more than 72 hours, and then it will be off to France. I had a swell time at home even though it was short. (Two hours instead of two weeks). I hope this finds you and Don alright and that you find a place to stay. Well, lots of luck and take care of yourself and maybe we will be home together soon. I'll write just as soon as I get my new address.

Lots love and kisses.

Bill

CHAPTER 8

Uncle Bill's Duty in the
European Theater

(JANUARY 1945—MAY 1946)

THESE LETTERS FROM MY MOM'S BROTHER, BILL, OFFERED us a window on the close of the European war through the eyes of our 25-year-old uncle, William T. Schubert, PFC. Whether it was his age, his denial, or his ignorance, he shared nothing about the potential combat he might be facing.

Finally, around the first of March, his company faced a surprise attack by the Germans. Afterward, he avoided talking to our Mom about it, saying he had already shared it with their own mother, clearly too traumatized to repeat the horrific stories. It turned out that two of Bill's best friends were severely wounded lying in a foxhole right next to him.

After the war ended, and Bill was in Germany with the occupation, he shared with Mom and his own mother that he was having reactions to the fire fight he had been in. He was diagnosed with nervous exhaustion in a hospital in Passau, Germany. He sounded very much like a soldier from today who is diagnosed with Post Traumatic Stress Disorder.

Bill's letters also described my parents' moves from Waco to Dallas in Texas, and finally to Salt Lake City, UT, during the first three months of 1945. Clearly, as they moved more quickly and further west, it became apparent that Dad was getting ready to be shipped out to the Pacific theater. Meanwhile, the war was coming to a close in Germany.

—————◆—————

January 31, 1945
Somewhere in England

Dear Don,

Just a short note to let you know that I am safe and sound somewhere in England. We had a wonderful crossing, did not get sick at all. Have you gotten a place to live yet, or are you still at the Grays' home in Waco? We expect to be moving again soon. By the radio and papers, it looks pretty good for us if the Russians keep going. I hope and pray that it will all be over before long so that we can all be home again. So long.

Bill

—————◆—————

February 14, 1945

Dear Jeanne

I am now in a hospital in Belgium with the slight case of the grippe. Nothing to worry about—been here for four days. So far, I have been pretty lucky in getting good bunks to sleep in and very good food. I hope I get back before our outfit pulls out, although I think they have pulled out already. I will be seeing you.

Bill

March 6, 1945

Dear Jeanne,

Just a few lines to tell you I am still in Germany. Wish I could write, but we are very busy these days. I am sure that Mother has told you what happened to me and our company. People are saying that the war should be over in two months. Lots of love and kisses.

Bill

March 27, 1945

Dear Jeanne,

Well, I finally got mail today. You mentioned in your letter about the nice place you had in Texas. Your "Victory" mail (no postage) of February 25 was sent from Dallas, so I see you that you are moving again. I see where your v mail of March 9 was sent from Salt Lake City. Take care of yourself.

Bill

CHAPTER 9

Dad Ordered West to Salt Lake City, Readying for the Pacific

(JANUARY 1945—MARCH 1945)

HOWEVER, BILL COPED WITH THE END OF THE WAR IN Europe, it was overshadowed by the reality of what he and Dad might eventually face in the Pacific. There is not much discussion in WWII histories about what the veterans of the European front were feeling after the Germans surrendered. There was both joyous celebration but more often a quiet thanksgiving on VE Day. Why? All able-bodied men in uniform in Europe realized that the war in the Pacific was far from over and that they would likely be sent there. Although a few of the island chains had been recaptured, they realized that an invasion of the Japanese mainland would take as long and be as difficult as winning back Western Europe from the Germans had been. Most rumors seemed to indicate that American troops would be directly transferred to the Pacific without any furlough or leave in the US.

Our parents left their car with friends in Omaha, NE, and took the train to Salt Lake City sometime in early March, not knowing when his orders to the Pacific would come. He had to spend most of his daylight hours at a post outside Salt Lake City, but he could usually get leave overnight. After dinner, he came to the Hotel Utah to be with Mom for the evening and overnight. It was his responsibility for organizing every detail of the entire troop train going west to an undisclosed location, but he didn't even know the date when he and thousands of others would have to leave.

On March 24, 1945, Dad arrived at the hotel on a six-hour leave, which he was able to share with Mom. The troop train he was responsible for organizing and coordinating was to leave for a yet-to-be-named embarkation depot on the west coast later that same evening. Although not going into direct combat, Dad was to travel over 10,000 miles around the world. Destination: unknown!

The following letters describe in detail how that evening was spent. However, the story of their actual goodbye was a tale that we heard many times as children in the 1950s, as adolescents in the 1960s and even well in the 1990s until Mom died in 1998.

After spending some intimate time together, they later shared in their letters that they hoped that a baby would result from their lovemaking. They had discussed in their almost four years of marriage of their desire to have kids. We were always left with the impression that they did not want to bring a child into the crazy world they were living in. But it turns out that they had tried but had not succeeded. Dad talked in a later letter of meeting an OB-GYN army officer who believed he knew why they had not succeeded. They shared how they looked forward to that day.

They each left Salt Lake City, hoping that they had produced a child. For about a month, the prospective baby was talked about in letters. But within a month, Mom shared that unfortunately this time there would be no baby.

After their private time, our parents decided to have one nice meal in the hotel dining room where they had the opportunity to dance together for one last time. Mom had decided that she did not want to go to the railroad station to say her final goodbyes. They did that in the hotel. And after Dad put his heavy pack on with all of his equipment hanging from his arms and shoulders, he headed straight down the street toward the station. Knowing that Mom, rather than taking the elevator back to her room, would walk up the fire stairs with windows in the hotel, every 100 yards, Dad would turn around and wave to Mom looking out the windows facing him. While he was walking, Mom would walk to the next floor—second, third, fourth, fifth, sixth, seventh, eighth, ninth—each time waving back at Dad as he slowly disappeared in the distance. Finally, on the tenth floor and at a corner, they both waved one last goodbye, having no idea if or when they would see each other again.

There's much more to the story, but my brother who had also heard the tale about Dad's leave-taking used this story in his remembrance at Mom's funeral in 1998. Her climbing the stairs at the Hotel Utah became a metaphor for meeting up with Dad in heaven whom she had last seen in June 1964. Having been married for 24 years and being separated for 34 years, they were together again.

Dad spent 48 hours in a deployment camp and then headed to San Francisco where he boarded the *SS Monterey*, a converted cruise ship, and one month later landed in Manila, Philippines. He did not see Mom for 375 days, until the spring of 1946, long after the war with Japan was over. Meanwhile, Mom headed back to Omaha on the train, where she picked up their car and drove alone back to her parents' home in Pennsylvania. Our parents' first letters to each other were written before dad left the US.

DON'S FIRST LETTERS TO JEANNE

March 28, 1946

My Darling,

Had your charming letters from Utah today. There is no possible expression I can use to describe how lovely—how

exciting—how uplifting they are. I, too, felt so completely uni-
fied by virtue of our Saturday night visit—our last in a while.
Nothing untoward happened; all went smoothly. No one knew
at all. And it was so, so delightful. At eight the next day, I was
thinking of you—hard and emotionally intense. You see, there
is a band playing! And bands bring tears. I cannot do justice
to your words. Suffice it to say, I have them and will treasure
them for the next few weeks by re-reading them and writing my
answers during a more contemplative period. Love,

 D

March 29, 1945

My Darling,

 I am well and happy, with plenty to eat, good sleep, and
missing you with every moment. We've been too busy to put it
into concrete thoughts. But soon, there will be time to think and
then missing you will be a physical— mental—all-consuming
thing. I shall attempt to phone you or wire you before you leave
Omaha. So difficult to write under these conditions. Hug and
kisses. I love you.

 D

March 30, 1945

Darling,

 I have been extremely busy. Things are moving fast, and
life is uncertain. We are at a camp on the west coast and if you
do not hear from me for a long time, do not worry. I am writing
to Chicago, so you will have a letter when you arrive.

I am going to miss you like crazy, but I'm not going to brood—I shall always be faithful. I shall always be dreaming of the day we shall be together again. Your letters will strengthen and provide fortitude for me; your prayers are distant inspiration. Your whispered words of love will be beacons out across the many miles like homing ranges to fliers. Hugs and Kisses.

I love you. D

JEANNE'S FIRST LETTERS TO DON

Hotel Utah
March 23, 1945

My loveliest Sweetheart,

What a beautiful three hours this has been. Somehow, I could send you off tonight without a tear, but this morning was miserable. How lucky we are to have had these extra hours of being together. Kisses, hugs, and love—so beautiful, so glorious that I can still feel the tenderness of your embrace, the first touch of you when we became a single oneness, and the glorious entrancing moment when it starts and the wheels submerge into a blinding ray of light, the most delightful of all, when I see the love in your eyes and feel the warmth of my dearest one's satisfaction. The little moments of this memory—your call—the rejoicing in your heart as I held you when you first came in—our love—and finally, watching as you walked down the street and the last goodbye wave before you rounded the corner and were out of sight. God bless you and keep you safe for me.

Your Punkin

Hotel Utah

March 24, 1945

My dearest Sweetheart,

You'll be so busy all morning getting your train in readiness that you may not get to call. What can I say, but "Do your job well and hurry back to me." I will come to you whenever and wherever you will want me. In the meantime, I shall keep the homes fires burning, saving all the money, so that we can start out anew in a little house of our own.

Don't ever worry about me. I shall always be okay, except to worry about you. It will be a job for both of us to do well—you abroad, I at home. And then we can team up again to do it together. I love you, my sweetheart.

Your Punkin

PART II

2000 Mile Weekly Missions

Atom Bombs and Surrender Excitement –
Waiting Months for Home and Punkin

(MARCH 1945–APRIL 1946)

CHAPTER 10

Dad Crosses the Pacific on the SS Monterey

(APRIL 1945)

SS. MONTEREY IS THE CONVERTED CRUISE SHIP THAT DAD TO THE
SOUTHWEST PACIFIC

SINCE MOM WAS AWARE THAT DAD WOULD BE 20 TO 30 DAYS on the ship with no mail, she wrote little notes and wrapped little presents, numbered them, and as the voyage continued, Dad would open one each day.

DAD'S LETTERS FROM THE *SS MONTEREY*

------------◆------------

April 4, 1945
Somewhere in the Pacific Ocean

Our Darling Punkin,

Of all the "Children's Crusades" you ever saw, this expedition to war is the most screwball of all. I cannot give any details, given censoring, but I can say there are many women passengers aboard. And such a "house party atmosphere you never saw." Singing and entertainment of one kind or another going on all the time! We get two meals daily. Beautiful, big seven-course dinners! Served in first class style at linen-covered tables. By regular stewards! There just isn't any connection between this trip and going to war. We were very lucky and drew a palatial cabin, private bath, tub, shower, big basin, and porcelain horse (toilet) with a green seat. Towels are furnished, beds made. Nothing to do all day but sit in the sun and contemplate the next whopping big meal. All we have to wash in, however, is cold sea water, so no one has taken an honest-to-goodness bath yet.

Today, I must take a sponge bath and put out a small wash. But you get so lazy. The sea air seems to do something to you and procrastination becomes a crowning virtue.

Our first day out was ROUGH! Even the old hands aboard allowed, as they hadn't seen the Pacific as rough in years. Many were sick. I, happily, was untroubled—ate our two meals and kept them! But at times, I was plenty apprehensive. Then on the next day, it smoothed out and I got my sea legs. Since then, I haven't even noticed the motion of the boat.

I haven't the slightest idea where this will be mailed from, but I'm getting it ready, just in case. I have another one also; that just missed the deadline at the staging area, so you'll have two from our first "real cutting-off place." I can't tell anything about our embarkation now, but it was quite wonderful—remember to ask all about it someday. I'm sure the impressions made will last indefinitely. I am writing this on deck on my knee and the breezes are gently blowing. Except for an occasional nap, life consists of sitting lazily in the sun gazing out into the blue. Song fests start spontaneously a dozen times a day—particularly after dinner at sundown—we are crowded in together like sardines; everyone has to get along with everyone else or go crazy. I should have an "automatic" mail delivery system. I told them I have a trained albatross, which flies like the wind —who makes a round trip from me to you each day carrying mail and other presents. When our poor albatross has to cross the International Date Line in his daily missions, I am indeed afraid for his sanity.

That's all for now. I must gather enough courage to take a cold salt-water bath and put out a small wash. I'll write again tomorrow. No ideas at all when this will go forward. Am well—happy, and I love you a thousand times a thousand.

Always yours,

Poppa

◆••••••••••••◆••••••••••••◆

April 11, 1945

Dear Punkin,

Today, I will open letter #2 and one other letter from my parents. They are lovely reminders and it was wonderful of you to organize them. I am quite the envy of our cabin-mates because I can be "more", and memories of our lovemaking give me such private pleasure. Our gang draws closer together as we approach our destination. Rooming with Hank. Everything developing in a very smooth manner.

Reading hundreds of letters daily as the censor for my company; almost the first one stabbed poignantly until the tears came. Such sadness in separation, multiplied a million-fold.

Since this trip began, I have a new-found respect for all GIs. These boys are a wonderful bunch. Sometimes coarse and hard, not refined, but steady, sure, and confident. Reading their letters is like reading a letter from your brother Bill a hundred times over. It is amazing that such men, so hard on the surface, can be so sensitive in their thoughts. Reading their letters is a sacred job, I feel.

◆ ·············· ◆ ·············· ◆

Friday, April 13, 1945

Dearest "the Mama,"

It is now noon on the Pacific, many miles from the USA. We have been going continuously more or less in a straight line at a considerable speed since exactly one week from the time I last saw the Punkin. In all that time, we have seen only one smidge of an island and that far off on the horizon. Anyone who has not made the crossing before has tremendous difficulty realizing the enormous stretches of the Pacific. As I mentioned in the last epistle, we are in equatorial waters, and it is unbearably hot and humid below decks. Each mealtime we sweat like bulls and rush back on deck to at least get the wonderful breeze.

◆ ·············· ◆ ·············· ◆

April 16, 1945
Somewhere in the Pacific

Darling Punkin,

After so many weeks of nothing, even the passing of a little harbor boat becomes an epochal event. Our family is getting better acquainted—it's so hot topside and so comfortable in our little cabin, we seem more and more to congregate here and thus gab more with each other. Our oldest is 39 and youngest 32 years old. We are from Kentucky, California, Wisconsin, Massachusetts, Ohio, South Carolina, Georgia, and, of course, Connecticut. All are majors. One Air Corps Communications man right out of the Pentagon; one in Chem Warfare, attached to the Air Corps; one in Airplane Maintenance; two dentists; and two medics. We have great gabs, with the medical officers and military officers offering very different opinions, but all with respect and kindness.

Love,
D

............◆............

April 17, 1945

My darling Punkin,

Here we are—almost halfway around the world—and finally our engines have come to a temporary halt. How long we will be here, nobody knows, but that we will not get to go ashore everybody knows. It is a pleasant change from the constant movement of the empty passing sea. Here in the harbor, we can keep our side bulkhead open at night as well as day. So, last night, we had our first fresh air sleep in a couple of weeks, and it was grand! But this morning, as soon as the sun came, it started to warm up and by now the sun is already devastating.

We are busy watching the little activity of this place. I cannot send a cable announcing safe arrival, but I can send one about feeling well and happy, which will mean that I have arrived safely. I love you even on the bottom side of the world.

  Love, D

              April 19, 1945

My Darling Punkin,

  Still in port somewhere in the Southwest Pacific. Been fussing around for two days or so putting off and taking on. Looks as though we're staying on and headed for some more sailing. It is not as cruelly hot as we imagined it would be. Seems to be a nice breeze, and at night, we don't have to button up for black-out. Started the Atabrine (to prevent malaria in the tropics). No yellow tinge yet. They say this is a nice place, but from what we can see of it, I'm sure glad we're staying on board to another place.

  I don't believe I told you that we are wearing fatigues all day. In our cabin, we wear nothing but our skivvies and slippers, shoes, or clogs. Consequently, we spend all day in the cabin. At first, we spent all day on the boat deck, but that has begun to pale, and our quarters are so fine that pretty soon, we wind up right back.

  Lonesome for you,

  D

              April 25, 1945

Dearly beloved,

  Somehow the days go by and we sail on and on, slower now, not at the breakneck speed we started out. Sunday and

Monday were unbearably humid and warm. Yesterday and today were more comfortable. The glittering moment of the day is at sunrise when we open after the blackout is over. We open the side wall sliding doors and take large draughts of fresh air. You can feel life flow back into your breath-starved body.

When I start a new numbering system, it will mean I finally reached a more or less permanent location. We cannot send a cable stating anything about arrival. However, I can send a "canned cable" stating I am well and happy as soon as I can after we arrive. I sure hope you will receive the mail we put off at the recent stop. Because I know it's been a long, long time. I am hungrily looking forward to a big batch of news and love when we finally catch up with the mail. Opened your #7 present. Also, Herb's letter with the pictures of their young ones—how cute they are! I put the pictures in my picture case.

In so doing, I looked at my pictures of the little ones and the doggie. We have had a wonderful five years together, my love. So many enchanted moments. And now I'm away from you— every ill-tempered word I've ever said seems to be an impossible thing, like a bad dream to be hurriedly forgotten. I'm sure that after this separation I can never be ill-humored with you again.

I started talking about the babies' picture, leading to our baby (ies)! When you are sure either way, please send me a canned cable. The uncertainty is cruel.

What do you hear from Bill? The 9th Army and all the rest are sure whipping Germany. By the 4th of July should see the end of organized resistance. We get the news each day by means of a ship's newspaper.

No poker today—the boys have tired of that too—I've been up and down a few pennies, but I got tired of it yesterday and quit in disgust. So now we sit—some good conversation at times—much arguing about military law—much bantering between Air Corp and Medical Corps.

I love you.

D

⋯⋯◆⋯⋯

April 27, 1945

My own darling,

Landfall again today. For a while, we thought we were sailing in circles, our rate of progress was so slow. But with the approach of islands we are apparently getting some place. I love you—my loveliest one. I never thought it would be this long.

Love,

D

⋯⋯◆⋯⋯

MOM HEADING EAST FROM SALT LAKE TO WICHITA— DRIVING TO CHICAGO AND PITTSBURGH

⋯⋯◆⋯⋯

LETTERS BELOW DESCRIBE THE RAIL JOURNEY MOM TOOK IN a Pullman car from Salt Lake City, through Cheyenne, WY, into Nebraska and finally to Omaha where friends and their 38 Pontiac were awaiting her. She spent a couple of days with her friends in Omaha but was rattled by two families and babies squeezed into war-time housing. Late night, writing to Dad, she described her dreams until she faced the aloneness of their separation.

Mom drove by herself through the rest of Nebraska into Iowa to spend the night in Cedar Rapids. She loved the rolling, now spring green hills and the feathery trees; she described Iowa as the nicest of all the Midwest states she had seen. Onward, she headed to Chicago to her aunt and uncle's home, where she was taken care of and kept busy. She didn't even have her coat off as she plowed into her letters from Dad.

March 26, 1945

Hello, my darling,

Back in my little cubicle, sitting and watching the plains of Nebraska roll by. Still quite a way to go to Omaha. No one was occupying the upper berth, so I was lolling in luxury: shoes off, feet up on the seat, pillow at my back, and dreaming of my dearest sweetheart. Finally, I fell asleep, dreaming of you. This morning, I awoke at 7.30, thinking of you, "Good morning, Sweetheart."

The German situation seems to be well in hand, looking at the morning papers. I have all the faith in the world that God will bring you and our Schubie-puss (her brother) home safely and then we can all start out anew.

The Punkin

April 1, 1944
Omaha, NE

Darling,

Funny ole momma that I am—somehow, I keep thinking there will some word for me to come to the West coast to meet you. Why do I persist in having that thought? I guess I still can't feel that you've gone. Perhaps you are on the boat by now and on the high seas. (Dad sailed the day before on March 31.)

With that feeling, there is such a strangeness in doing things alone now. It was noticeable on the trip to Omaha. Ordering my own dinner—carrying my own bags—in other words, on my own. And I don't relish it—but such little memories of our doing things together only make me see how closely interwoven my life has become with yours—how we really have become a single oneness—life will go on though, while we're apart but not until you return to me will it be so sweet and precious as it has been.

❖ ⋯⋯⋯ ◆ ⋯⋯⋯ ❖

In the first week of April 1945, the Germans surrender to the Russians on the Elbe River and meet the Americans from the West.

April 12, 1945: The Americans and the rest of the world are stunned with the news that President Franklin D. Roosevelt has died at Warms Springs, GA.

❖ ⋯⋯⋯ ◆ ⋯⋯⋯ ❖

April 13, 1945
Chicago

Darling,

It was such a pleasant day with good news—until the first shocking news came over the radio at 5:10 p.m. How many millions like us were stunned with the news that our leader President Roosevelt had passed away. Unashamedly, I wept openly. Many hearts are heavy tonight. Even I, who never knew him, feel such a tremendous loss. The one man in who we believed, who we placed our trust to bring us through this chaos, no longer is here. What is to happen now? There is no doubt in my mind that the Allies will go on to victory. But after that. What? What man have we to see that peace has really been achieved? So many thoughts, so many questions are in the minds of everyone tonight. Only time will tell the story. But somehow, you and I, along with others, will go on and do our part to see that peace and freedom do prevail throughout the world once this war has been won. In our hearts, there is the conviction that the little people like you and me are the ones to carry on his crusade for world peace.

Love,

Punkin

◆ · · · · · · · · · · · · ◆ · · · · · · · · · · · · ◆

Three days later

April 15, 1945

Chicago

My Sweetheart,

The past three days have been gray ones indeed and my heart has been heavy. How I wish I could paint in words the picture of "the man on the street" during the past 72 hours. It makes one humble to think that so many people could feel the loss of one man. How great a trust had been placed in him!

Somehow though, I feel as one man said today over the radio, "President Roosevelt was a great man while living, but in death he will be greater." Yes, I can see it that way already. The feeling has spread that the American people are reunited. United as never before in their determination to carry on his job and see it becomes a reality and not just a dream.

The San Francisco Conference (creating the United Nations) goes on as scheduled. Premier Molotov and Foreign Secretary Eden will be there. And today, word came that Poland will accept the decisions as laid down at the Yalta Conference.[4] Perhaps, this is boring you, but when one has felt nothing but confusion and question for three days, the mind is hard put to consider lighter things.

---

4   Somewhat odd that this daughter of Polish immigrants approved of the Soviet domination of Poland. It is my un-derstanding that this decision by a very sick and exhausted Roosevelt was the beginning of the Cold War.

Today's news has been quite eventful. So, Russia has broken her pact with Japan. There is much to be hoped for in that act, for while it is not an open declaration of war on Japan, it looks like hostilities will begin between them. If so, the hope springs up in our hearts that with Russia's help in the war, Bill will be home soon.

Love from your Punkin.

* * *

Late April 1945: Various German armies surrender to US and Soviet troops.

Later in April 1945, many Allied forces liberate a number of concentration camps throughout Germany and Eastern Europe.

The insanity of the Final Solution becomes known to the world.

April 30, 1945: Hitler and his partner, Eva Braun, commit suicide in his bunker.

Germany surrenders on May 8, 1945.

May 9, 1945 is declared VE Day.

CHAPTER 11

Uncle Bill Faces Trauma as the War Ends in Europe

(FEBRUARY 1945-AUGUST 1945)

DURING APRIL AND MAY 1945, MOM ONLY RECEIVED ONE letter from her brother, and it said nothing about Bill being in combat with the Germans, although April was the last full month of the war. Finally, in late May, she received a Victory mail from Bill. He mentioned nothing about combat but seemed to be suffering from depression and anxiety about what he had gone through, but, more importantly, what his near future might be: shipped to the Pacific Theatre.

Mail delivery on the European front, given combat conditions, remained spotty at best. Sometimes it would be three months between letters. On one day, Bill would receive 57 letters. And it appeared that even after the war ended, it did not get much better.

Although Bill's mother, my grandmother, would have known what happened in those six to eight weeks, all she ever said was Bill had a tough combat experience and never really talked about it. Our impression as his nephews was that he was a very subdued guy. He did have eight kids, and he supported them and his wife as a machinist for Westinghouse Air Brake, living a block from where he grew up in East McKeesport, PA—just a few moments of joy and happiness in an otherwise generally sad life, a casualty of the war.

❦

May 20, 1945

Dear Jeanne,

Well, I finally got up enough ambition to write a few letters, so here goes. I guess you read in my letter to mother of my experiences over here, so I won't go into it for now. . . We are doing guard duty in a small town near Stendhal, Germany. Well, as far as my staying over here as part of the Army of Occupation, that is out. Tomorrow, we take our physical exam for the Pacific, and I doubt, very much, we will get a furlough. General Simpson, head of the 9th Army, asked right out for our division, the 102nd Division, so that is why I doubt if I will get a furlough before going to the Pacific.

Have you had a chance to see Mary yet? Maybe you can find out what is up with her? I haven't received a letter from her in a long time. [5] Lots of luck and write soon. Lots of love and kisses.

Bill.

PS. I'll write to Don tomorrow night.

❦

---

5   Mary was his 18-year-old girlfriend back in PA whom my mom and grandmother visited at Bill's request since she had stopped writing to him. He eventually came home to marry her.

June 25, 1945

Dear Jeanne,

Just a note to let you know I am doing OK. We are still right outside Erfurt and will be moving 160 miles southwest of here in about a week or 10 days. We are now attached to the 7th Army. The latest report is that our division will be split up. The men who have less experience like me will be sent directly to the Pacific. Have not heard about the teaching job. I had been asked whether I wanted to be a teacher in a military training school in England. Say hello to Don's folks. Lots of love and kisses.

Bill

* * *

June 29, 1945

Dear Don,

I am getting along all right. My CO asked me to work on the demonstration programs for the education program, over here, several weeks ago, I was asked to instruct in the machinist line, but so far haven't heard anything on it. They won't get the education program going until they know who will be in the army of occupation. Lots of luck and take care of yourself.

Bill

* * *

July 10, 1945

Dear Jeanne,

Just a few lines to tell you I am getting along fine and hope you are. How is the weather in New London? It is very warm here and lots of rain. We are in a village about 10 miles from the border with Austria. We are in the 3rd Army and are in one of the 18 divisions, which will be here until January 1946. For the past few days, I have been horseback riding in the evenings after doing guard duty or drilling. We haven't had mail in over two weeks. Take care of yourself and write.

Bill

--------------◆--------------

July 20, 1945

Dear Don,

Just how does the South Pacific agree with you? How are you getting along? How long do you think the war will last? President Truman is now in Berlin with Stalin and Churchill. Boy, they sure must be giving Japan hell. Almost as bad as Germany was given. Several rumors are that Stalin has an unconditional surrender with Japan and will act as the go-between Japan and the US. Another rumor is that Russia will start an offensive against Manchuria as the conference is over. Here's hoping that at least one of them is true. Russia attacking Japan will shorten the war considerably. Our platoon and our weapons' platoon have been chosen to be the lead platoon for our entire division over the next six weeks. Hope to hear from you soon.

Bill

--------------◆--------------

July 28, 1945

Dear Jeanne,

Nothing much to report except that I went to Passau this week to see the USO show with Jack Benny, Ingrid Bergman, and Larry Adler. It was pretty good. I am glad I took my field glasses, or I wouldn't have seen anything as we were so far back. Mail delivery is still bad—over two weeks. They have been cutting *down on our rations recently. Take good care of yourself and write soon. Lots of love and kisses.*

Bill

◆············◆············◆

August 4, 1945

Dear Jeanne,

I went on sick call last Thursday to get a physical check-up. They sent me to a hospital in Passau, and the last couple of days, I have been having a number of tests. They think I have neuro-circulatory asthma. Do you know what that is? I should be getting the results back tomorrow. So, I will write you to tell you what the results are. It's been getting chilly here, especially when it rains. Can you send me a box of food? They are still cutting down our rations. Lots of love and kisses.

Bill

◆············◆············◆

August 7, 1945

Dear Jeanne,

How is everything doing out there on the coast? I finally got the results of the tests and will probably leave the hospital tomorrow. I am in pretty good shape except for a slight case of nervousness, which, in turn, causes me to have a sharp pain in the heart now and then, but nothing to worry about, and there is nothing they can do to stop the pain. I cannot wait to get back to my company to see if I have some mail or some packages.

It has warmed up today. I hope it stays that way, so I can go swimming when I get back. Please send me a package of food. I am starving. Lots of love and kisses.

Bill

◆·············◆·············◆

September 8, 1945

Dear Jeanne,

By the time this letter reaches home, you will be back, so I hope you had a good trip back and that you and mother enjoyed it. Yesterday, I got 57 letters and my head is spinning from reading them. Well, anyway here goes. Teaching begins next week, and we will be ready. No further news on promotion yet. We will get our weekends off and also our evenings, so that part is good. I tried to send home a couple of German officers' uniforms and a couple of knives or swords but didn't work.

As for the photographs, we had to carry the films with us and after the war ended, we set up our own studio and developed and printed them. As for the horse incident, well, the horse didn't see the ditch; therefore, when his front feet hit it, he just went down, nothing serious. Don't send any more food or magazines. We now have plenty of food and we have all kinds of reading material here in England, not like in Germany. We didn't swim in the Danube River, but we were on boats and fished a little. We arrived in London on August 14 and we got into camp late that night, but we slept through all the excitement. The only day I'll celebrate is the day I get my discharge papers. Last week, I went up to Barrow and spent a wonderful time with a girl I met in Blackpool the week before last. They treated me swell and it reminded me a lot of home. I slept in a bed with white sheets, boy, the first time for quite a while. They want me to come up anytime I get a chance too or maybe I'll take them up on it, only I won't take advantage of them. I'll send you a picture of Doris. She is a very enjoyable girl and can really dance. I got my civilian shoes and they sure feel good. Lots of love and kisses.

Your brother, Bill.

CHAPTER 12

Mom's Tough Adjustment to Life
Alone in Pittsburgh

(APRIL — JUNE 1945)

MOM'S MOTHER TRAVELED TO CHICAGO TO HER SISTER'S TO meet Mom and drive back with her to Pittsburgh. After a few days' visit, they took off on April 21 and stopped in Cleveland, OH, for the night. Cleveland, the city where Dad worked during much of the 1930s, was one home base he had much love for. They took off on April 22 and arrived home in East McKeesport, PA, late that afternoon, an 1,800-mile train and road trip from Salt Lake City.

Home just three days, Mom realized the void and emptiness she began to feel after the bustle and excitement of traveling and being with people. East McKeesport was no longer her home. Her days were half-filled with cooking and keeping house for her parents who were working two jobs and unpacking and organizing all that had been shipped home from the Midwest and Reading. But this did not fill up the days of loneliness and sadness.

Mom and her mom and dad also spent a lot time worrying about Bill, her brother and their son. The war was ending in Europe, but they were anxious about Bill, who would probably be transferred immediately to someplace in the Pacific. Though he had not been physically hurt in Europe, they were concerned about the impact of the trauma he would suffer if he were to face combat again.

••••••••••••••••◄━►••••••••••••••

April 23, 1945
E. McKeesport, PA

Dearest Sweetheart,

Last night, after I had gone to bed, how deeply it struck me that my poppa was so far away, and it would be a long time before I would see him again.

Perhaps because these past four weeks have been filled with busy days and being among strangers, I didn't fully recognize how empty and void my life was. But now I am home, I can "let my hair down." Now I must begin to plan for the days that lie ahead; it's no longer a life on a merry-go-round; it's for days of waiting for the first mail from you—days of waiting until you are home again with me. And so, I was unhappy last night.
Love, Punkin

••••••••••••••••◄━►••••••••••••••

April 25, 1945
East McKeesport, PA

Darling,

While I am glad to be at home with Mom and Dad to help them through these critical days regarding Bill, I still feel at loose ends, for it is not like being in our own home where I could be going ahead with fixing things for your return. Yet, that is something that I want you to share, establishing our own little house and fixing up things together.

I can remember the first months you went away in 1942 to Miami Beach and then Enid. How irritable and how nasty and mean I was. But you were the patient and gentle and under-standing one who helped me through the first weeks when I came to you. How many times I hurt you? Oh, I remember them all, my sweetheart, for they hurt me, too. But I learned my lessons well. Your Punkin.

❖ ┄┄┄ ━ ┄┄┄ ❖

Finally, Mom got her first letters from Dad.

❖ ┄┄┄ ━ ┄┄┄ ❖

April 27, 1945
E. McKeesport, PA

Dearest Sweetheart,

Though the skies were cloudy and gray this day, my heart has been gay, and I've had a song on my lips. For today came my first mail from wonderful poppa.

Two letters! Darling, you can't imagine how life has changed since 4 o'clock this afternoon.

All my love,
Your Punkin

CHAPTER 13

Dad's Year of Service in the Pacific Begins

(MAY 1945 — MARCH 1946)

DAD ARRIVED AT A REASSIGNMENT CAMP NEAR MANILA ON May 2. He sat in the hot sun without anything to do for over 10 days. He did not know where he would be assigned or how long he would be in the Pacific. After two weeks, he was finally assigned to be a traveling inspector based out of Hollandia, Dutch New Guinea. This assignment meant that each week he would travel 2,000 miles across the ocean and back again, stopping at various bases on the many recaptured islands to do inspections as part of the Inspector General's office.

So, Dad and Mom sent each other close to 300 letters over the next year that Dad was away. Some letters would take as little as seven days to go 10,000–13,000 miles from Pittsburgh, PA, to the Pacific Islands, where Dad was serving. Ironically, the time lag for letters worsened after the Japanese surrender on September 2, 1945. As the War Department tried to get servicemen home, there were fewer mechanics to service the fewer planes. This reduction resulted in delays of mail, sometimes taking over two weeks to get a letter from the US to the far Southwest Pacific. The morale of the men who were left behind on all these islands suffered dramatically the longer they had to stay with no real mission after the Japanese surrendered and with no news from home.

Given these varying travel times for mail, it was impossible to keep the letters in any exact order of when they were read and answered. In fact, seldom did Dad write a letter and my mom answer that specific letter or vice versa. However, Mom was very careful about the order of the letters that she wrote (#1, #2, etc., on each letter). Dad was less careful and would sometimes forget to number his letters. For all these reasons, I have kept the letters chronologically grouped by months and author from May 1945 to March 1946. A month's letters will become a chapter in the memoir.[6]

As in any correspondence, you will begin to see them responding to each other's questions or feelings or ideas. They tell a great love story between Poppa and his Punkin! Moreover, there will be less of my narrative about this year in the Pacific. Mom and Dad's own words will tell their story.

Only included are those letters that give the reader some insight into my parents', grandmother's, and uncle's reaction to the historical events of the time period; their feelings that changed throughout the year, given their loneliness or isolation; their strategies that kept them busy and occupied during their separation; the struggle to live under rationing; and finally how even 10,000 miles apart, they worried about their families, specifically about their own parents who were aging at home with less income and high inflation.

---

6   It is clear that our grandmother (dad's mom) also writes almost as often as my mom. It is a shame that far less than 50 of these 300 letters survive since my dad had very little dry space to store even my mom's letters. These 50 somehow survive because my dad includes them in his let-ters to my mom and my mom saves all of the letters, my dad's, my grandmother's, and her broth-er's.

TELEGRAM TO MOM ANNOUNCING DAD'S SAFE ARRIVAL IN PHILIPPINES

DAD'S LETTERS (MAY 1945)

THIS FIRST MONTH OF LETTERS REFLECTED THAT ALMOST all of the men, including Dad, had never lived in a tropical environment. Having come from the luxury of the ship and now being quartered in temporary facilities, their complaints were real, the first shocks of being "in the field." My Dad seemed to realize that but sitting on a canvas cot for two to three weeks with nothing to do in a hostile environment was reflected in these first month of letters. Finally, Dad was assigned to the Administrative Inspection HQ in Hollandia, Dutch New Guinea, as a traveling inspector. Each week he flew to various small or large Army Air Corps bases all over the South Pacific, logging 1,500 to 2,000 miles a week for the next few months. He was constantly on the move. My mom shared some worries about his flying so much across thousands of miles of open water. As kids, we were only told that he was in the Philippines in the war, but this point of view must have given him a much broader perspective on the war, especially since he was inspecting Army Air Corps facilities.

＊⋯⋯⋯⋯＊⋯⋯⋯⋯＊

May 8, 1945

Somewhere in the Pacific

A good morning note to you. I haven't been able to cable any word yet. We are on the lookout for a place to send a cable and may find one today. Things are rough in this area. War becomes real at last. I can't describe it to you in this letter.

We are perfectly safe —no air raids—no possibility of ambush, but it hasn't been that way very long. I gather we are in plenty of time to see the pictures for next week's newsreel.

Love, D

＊⋯⋯⋯⋯＊⋯⋯⋯⋯＊

May 7, 1945, 5 p.m.

My darling Punkin,

Here I am again today: Much better mood tonight. I am lying down on my bunk. About 1 or 2 p.m., I was at a complete low. It was unbearably hot—with a breeze like from an oven. Under the tent, my fever stick showed 104 degrees. My own temp was only 100.2. We had a miserable lunch—there was no news about assignments. There are sound rumors that we'll get our orders tomorrow and most wonderful of all—mail call brought two letters from you.

So, my mood has undergone a complete reversal—wonderful letters almost made me cry with aching for you. At night, I wake up from these dreams of you and the loneliness overwhelms me. During the day, I seem to get along, but the nights are awful. Of course, I go to sleep at 8 p.m. but about midnight I wake up and lay awake for an hour or so brooding over our separation. Love, D

May 8, 1945

My Darling Punkin,

I haven't had a cup of coffee since Friday morning 6 a.m. For breakfast, we had TEA again, canned corned beef diluted with water—prunes, bread, and butter. If we don't get out of this dump pretty soon, I'm going to starve to death. Everybody is bitching and screaming. Our Lt. Col. is just itching to get assigned, so we can inspect the joint and blow it wide open.

Our assignments are supposed to have been in since the day before we arrived—and still we sit stewing, waiting for someone to cut an order. It isn't living in the field that gets us provoked—it's living in the field when we're equipped for a 10,000-mile journey of two years' duration but do nothing— with nobody giving a damn.

Love, D

May 9, 1945

My dearly beloved,

Another stultifying day of complete inactivity and utter aimlessness as we swelter under our tents. Our IG Deputy Lt. Col. is fit to be tied. If he doesn't make somebody's bottom burn for this when he gets into action, I miss my guess.

We've had no war news the last three days except for scraps of rumors that Germany has capitulated with unconditional surrender. Please be sure to send clippings of the front page of the NY Times when big things are happening.

Love, D

May 10, 1945

My Dearly Beloved,

Now we come to that quiet time of the day when I have had a shower and life seems almost tolerable and I can contemplate a letter to my love. First, the joyful: I got two letters from Punkin—#24, from April 26, and #25, from April 27, and four v mails from my momma, dated April 12, 13, 14, and 16.

Second, the food was considerably better today but still no coffee, and lastly, it's been much cooler. Now the sad: our little family is broken up. Out of 42 of us that have been together since March 5, only about 10 of us are left and five or so may be out tomorrow. Most of my particular buddies went along, including Hank (a friend from Garden City), bless his heart. I don't know why I hadn't mentioned him before. We've been together quite often. Roomed together in the staging area on the West Coast. But now he is gone and with so many with whom I made lasting friendships, but the army was ever thus.

My own circumstances are in an unhappy aspect. There is a hitch in the assignment. I have been assigned to Headquarters Far East Air Service Command—APO 323. That, however, is located in a place distant from where I now am.[7] But they have a branch office located in the vicinity of this depot. Thus, before they decide what to do, they must consult the distant HQ I am assigned, by wire. This will take maybe a week—SOOO, I guess we must be philosophical. Anyway, food is better and there is more room to move around in this tent now that some have left. You mentioned something about my letters not being censored. Only a few will be probably. Officers censor their own mail and sign that it is OK. Just a few spot checks.

Love, D

---

7   It is actually 1,840 miles south of the Philippines in Hollandia, Dutch New Guinea.

‹············—············›

May 11, 1945

My dearly beloved,

Once again, we come to that cool, delightful, refreshing part of the day just before sundown. If I only had a long, tall cool glass of water, I'd be fairly content. It's amazing how rapidly we adapt ourselves, though. During the day, water is in the Lister bags for drinking, and it gets very warm. I'd say about 80 to 90 degrees, whereupon its foulest taste comes to the fore and it tastes like 100 octane gasoline. The second day we experimented with a device, which keeps it nice and cool through the day. We take a sock and place a canteen with warm water in the sock. Then we soak the sock with water, warm, even hot. Then we hang the canteen in the shade where the breeze will evaporate the wet sock. Lo and behold, in about an hour, the water in the canteen is cool and palatable. So, our days are built around trips to the Lister bags for canteens of water and helmets of water to soak the canteen.

Today, I went wandering down by the bay. I found a headquarters, which now must be nameless. It is situated in an old estate—has some beautiful grounds around—right on the water's edge. One large house with red marble floors in the main building. Between it and the beach is a white tile swimming pool, not in operation, but the pavilion around it was a beautiful place. I can imagine how those stationed there can, after a hot day's work, relax in the sea breeze under the stars and listen to the water rolling on the beach. This place was mercifully spared. Houses on all sides are ugly, charred ruins, bombed and shelled to hell and gone. But surrounding this estate for one block are similar houses not quite as fancy as the main house. There were lilacs and red bougainvillea bushes in abundance. Even in the mid-day heat, their delightful odor was noticeable.

Love, D

• • • • • • • • • • • • —◆— • • • • • • • • • • • •

May 12, 1945

Dearest Beloved,

Here are my orders. I told you I felt lucky today. Got the orders to get going this afternoon. That's all I can tell you now. I mentioned that Post 323 is some distance from here in my previous letter.

Love, D

• • • • • • • • • • • • —◆— • • • • • • • • • • • •

May 13, 1945

Darling,

Here is a note from 10,000 feet above somewhere in the Southwest Pacific.

Any resemblance between the mode of travel and an airplane in the States is strictly nil. Bucket seats line the sides and we are herded helter-skelter with baggage piled around us, about up to our eyes. The trip has been very comfortable on the whole—quite smooth. You will be interested, and no doubt derive considerable fiendish pleasure from the fact that in the past 24 hours I have had two sandwiches, two doughnuts, and two cups of coffee.

What a time we had getting out of the Hellhole! First, we had a torrential downpour and thunderstorms. At about 2 a.m., there was four inches of water underneath my cot. Happily, everything that was packed was on top of other cots, so nothing was soaked. Then, at our time of departure, well before dawn, came a repeat performance. One other lad and I are making the journey, and we went over to the motor pool to find our transportation to the field, and the jeep was stuck in the mud. We made it. All of it was sheer downright fun because we had an opportunity to get out of that Replacement joint.

I am sitting with my field overcoat buttoned up around my neck with gloves on. As we were soaking wet this a.m., we went up high in the cold. I'd thought we'd die before I could get to my footlocker at the first stop to get the coat out. No breakfast. But again, I say—we took it in our stride, rejoicing to be on our way.

Love you, my Punkin,

D

⋅⋅⋅⋅⋅⋅⋅⋅⋅⋅⋅⋅⋅⋅⋅⋅⋅⋅⋅⋅⋅⋅⋅⋅

May 14, 1945

Darling my beloved,

I am the happy one tonight. We arrived safely at our new station, almost 1,800 miles from the Philippines back in the Southwest Pacific. It was arduous—no food from Saturday a.m. to Monday noon. When we arrived, we were sorry looking soldiers. But so happy to be situated at a place where I belong—I can begin to build an entity and not be a transient. We've had two good meals already. They have a nice officer's club with Cokes, 24 cans of beer a month and four cartons of cigarettes a month. Our barrack is on a frame of two-by-fours with a corrugated iron roof, well screened, electric lights, cement floor, two showers, and wash basins with the safest cool water. All of the men seem to be cordial, pleasant, and helpful. Tomorrow, I report to the Inspector for an interview, and then I can cut my teeth into a job and get busy with this war.

Love,

D

* ············· ◆ ············· ◆

May 15, 1945

Somewhere in Dutch New Guinea

My Wonderful Darling,

 Today, I sat at a desk and read regulations—first time in four months—and did it feel good. I'm only temporarily here, to hang my hat until they make up their minds as to the specific assignment.

 Today, Captain Welsh in the Inspector's office heard from his wife in Texas; a letter mailed one week ago! So that means the mail service is pretty good.

 Had another beautiful shower after work tonight—cold as the dickens—right from up on the mountain. We have a peak right straight up from the camp—2,000 feet taller than the tallest one in Pennsylvania. It has waterfalls that we can see way up there.

Love,

D

* ············· ◆ ············· ◆

May 18, 1945

Somewhere in Dutch New Guinea

My own Darling,

 Tonight, our little transient cabin has been augmented by four fly colonels going from somewhere to somewhere else. All the old hands have been gabbing away at a great rate about conditions here and in Australia and New Caledonia in 1942. I sit back and take it in. Conditions must have been grim indeed.

In fact, I think it would hasten the war if they would immediately send all the men home who are here for over 30 months. They have lost something—even those with 24 months should go because they have, for the most part, gone stale—no disrespect to them. They have just been away too long—been tropicalized. They are tired, both physically and mentally. This horrible life, its monotony, its bad food, its lack of any kind of home—even a hut or a tent—where you can settle down until they have gone stale. Just like a football team that's over-trained. They bicker, they fuss, they "back-bite." They can't see the forest for the trees. They spend so much time bitching about the difficulties of doing a job there's no time to do the job. Enlisted men and officers have done their part and should go home and let us green horns carry the ball.

Love,

D

May 21, 1945

My dearest one,

Tonight, it's humid and I have a lather on just sitting on my cot. I can understand how these guys get lazy and have a "don't care" attitude after 30 months in this climate. Particularly under conditions where you never get a nice starched clean uniform, and even if you had one, there'd be no place to wear it except right where you've been every seven days for every week. I suppose they snap back as soon as they hit civilization again but there is a cynical, cantankerous, belly-achin' bunch while they are here.

I love you.

D

May 22, 1945

Darling,

...To roll the enemy back these huge distances in this god-forgotten country. It's hard to realize but it's nearly 4,000 miles from Brisbane to Manila and another 1,000 nearly to Okinawa, the present forward area. And once after leaving "the continent," or the mainland as they call Australia, there isn't a 100-mile stretch of motor highway or railroad to be used for movement of supplies over the whole damn route. The logistics problem is almost wholly "aquatic or aerial." And every guy, whose face is yellow from Atabrine, who is tired from fatigue of the mind, whose élan and spirit are wet as a dishrag from lack of clean fresh clothes and any association with girls is deserving of the utmost sympathy—they sometimes now act like spoiled children.

That's why I hate to see troops moving from Europe over here after the German surrender. It doesn't seem right to cause them to risk their lives again and again in another theater. When they are so tired of it all. And when they get here, they'll be no damn good because of fatigue. These newspaper stories of how all the army in Europe wants to be over here to get at the Japs is poppycock to the average soldier. No man in his right mind who has been 24 months here wants to go anywhere but home. And they've lost their efficiency and eagerness to such a point that the course of the war is slowed down, in my opinion, by using them instead of fresh troops. Just my opinion. I've only seen a minuscule part of the whole picture. These men who have done a magnificent thing should be allowed to rest.

Love,

D

May 23, 1945

Darling,

In response to Mr. Roosevelt's death, we had the news very promptly. It seemed incredible and we do not fully realize it because of our unusual surroundings and lack of newspapers. There was a memorial service on Sunday afterwards. Hank went and said it was extremely inadequate—almost revolting in its "corniness."

Love,

D

May 24, 1945

Darling,

This evening, the cold shock of reality of our separation came over me, the long dull train ride to Miami and Miami Beach, the eight weeks of "hay foot—straw foot", and the 4th of July when the lovely one came down to see me—our wonderful week together. Separation on our anniversary at Jacksonville. When this is over, pray God, let us never be separated over 24 hours again. Three long years in the Army and now look, 10,000 miles apart, half a world away. I am sad tonight on this, my Army birthday. Rather than something to look forward to, there is infinitesimal recompense for this being without you and civilization. Damn the old Japs anyway—why don't they up and quit.

I have been reading the May 14 issue of TIME magazine that I mentioned. It described VE Day. How "cheated" I felt. The great gratitude and thankfulness, the celebration, the exultations at the Victory were stolen from me as I sat for the days in question sweating and rotting away on a cot in an oven-like tent in the Philippines. Completely apart and out of this world, we didn't even know what was going on.

A historic moment that the world will long remember passed by, out of sight down the other side of the hill. The hill that is the curvature of the broad Pacific. Now reading about it, it seems such an ineffectual anti-climax. Here was a moment that years were pointed toward, and it slipped through my hand like sand. They'll be another V day soon, a VJ day, and maybe we over here in the forgotten theater will have our exultation and experience the joy of attaining the mission.

People are funny here. There is a sad, hangdog, depressed quality, a forlorn expression of having been forgotten in most of the older hands. It makes the new ones of us lose our eagerness and our buoyancy. We become self-conscious at the display of semblance of our own autonomy, aggressiveness, and vitality.

Love,

D

May 26, 1945

My Darling,

...Up until now we have not even gotten the war news. Now though because we get the radio news broadcast on the boys' radios in the barracks, we don't feel so much adrift. But there is still that awful lonely feeling even in the midst of groups of people at the office, club or mess, or in the barracks. It is a stifling, stultifying thing—like something bad has you in its trap. You can't get away, no matter how.

I notice you are working hard, organizing our belongings back in PA. Don't overdo it. Finally, at long last, all of our things are together in one place. I wonder where they'll go next. We have surely been gypsies in our five years, haven't we? Our wonderful love. Our blessed memories will sustain us in our hours of loneliness. Most of the time I think, "Surely, this war cannot go on longer." But some other times, I see the mammoth job ahead in terms of logistics, of time, manpower, and equipment it takes to wage a war and I shudder with fright at the thought of not getting home for two or three years.

Love,

D

◆ ⋯⋯⋯⋯⋯ ◆ ⋯⋯⋯⋯⋯ ◆

May 29, 1945

My Wonderful Punkin,

Went to movies last night at the Officer's Club. Saw "Tonight and Every Night." I enjoyed the color, the glamorous dresses the dances, music, and songs. One can almost starve to death for wanting that kind of beauty in one's life...

I got a new title. I am Assistant Chief, Administrative Inspection Branch, Office of the Air Inspector, HQ, Far East Air Service Command. Ain't that a dilly? It's a lot of malarkey. Actually, I'm a flunky and that's OK until I catch on a little more to the peculiarities of this new command. Right now, there's a clash of personalities in the office like crazy. Happily, it has nothing to do with me. And I get along with all hands—at least so far. Fortunately for all hands, most of the folks are on the road, most of the time flying between islands. So, all stays serene.

Love, D

MOM'S LETTERS (MAY 1945)

◆ · · · · · · · · · · · ◆ · · · · · · · · · · · ◆

May 1, 1945

Darling,

... Mother and I went to the movies and saw "Kismet" last night. Quite colorful and enjoyable. And I was especially glad we went, for they showed a resume of President Roosevelt's four terms in office—giving the highlights of his career. How little did we realize what a terrific burden he had been carrying and what a physical change had been wrought upon him. It made your heart ache to see him so.

Today, the news has been entirely about the purported death of Hitler and the allied invasion of Borneo. And I was thinking of you so much, wondering if perhaps your assignments might lead to being sent there since Borneo is definitely in the equatorial zone. I try not to worry about you, yet I cannot help but worry. And when I look at the map and see how much still remains to be reconquered from the Japs, it looks like an awfully long and big job ahead.

Love,

Your Punkin

◆ · · · · · · · · · · · ◆ · · · · · · · · · · · ◆

May 2, 1945

Darling,

...Your job is yet to be completed; yet in your hearts, you must have experienced some joy and thanksgiving that victory in Europe or rather that fighting has ceased on the Western Front. Yes, VE Day has come! Our family rejoices, for it means that our Bill is spared for a little while longer. Yet, we know the

tasks and problems that lie ahead in Europe will be just as great, if not greater than the securing a military victory.

Already, people have put aside this part of the war and their thoughts are turned to the war with Japan. Still, it would have done your heart good to have seen the manner in which people reacted. None of this rabid frenzied rejoicing, but a quiet thankfulness was on the faces of people as you saw them on the street. Tonight, for the services at church, people thronged in droves. Never have I seen the church filled so. And it raised one's spirits up to see that groups of men and women gathered together to celebrate the victory in that manner.

Love to my darling,
Punkin

※ .... ◆ .... ◆

May 5, 1945

My dearest one,

Just two hours ago came your cable saying you were safe in the Philippines and you had received letters up through April 18. It was so wonderful to get the cable, for I had been thinking of you constantly for the past few days, thinking that you had surely reached some destination by this time. All that time no doubt your word of arrival was on its way here.

I am so glad, Darling, that you are somewhere I can fix my point of vision, if you understand what I mean. I wonder now how long it will before you received your assignment: what will it be and where you may be sent. Right now, I am speculating just where in the Philippines you may be. But I shall not worry, knowing you have safely reached this point.

My poor Dad was so upset when the boy came to the door saying he had a telegram. Naturally, his first thoughts went to Bill. But he was happy to hear it was from you.

I put in a call to your Momma right away and got her almost immediately. So, she now knows too. She was so glad I called and excited to hear that you had arrived. I didn't get to speak to Dad; he must have been resting. But I hope the good news helps to pep him up, for Mom says he hadn't been feeling too well of late. Maud came home from Boston Hospital on Thursday; she is getting along just fine—still using crutches, but there is no sign of any limp at all. I think that is just wonderful.

Now, I shall be looking forward to receiving some mail from you pretty soon and having it come in rather regularly. There are so many things I would like to know, but I shall leave that up to you to tell me what you can and save the rest for a later date. Mother and Dad send their love and ask me to tell you they are glad to hear of your safe arrival. I shall write an Air Mail tomorrow; both of these letters will not go until Monday. All my bestest love.

The Punkin

◆ ············· ◆ ············· ◆

May 12, 1945

My darling,

Your V mail of May 1 arrived on Saturday morning, May 12. It was so good to get word from you. It doesn't look like my Poppa is billeted at the Royal Palms Hotel!!! No more roast beef—from now on its Spam. Looks like you will not have to wait too long for your assignment, if you are packed to go places. Now I am worried that you will be sent some place where you cannot tell me about, and I shall wear myself down to the bone trying to figure it out. As I wrote last week, I had called Momma when your cable arrived. Today, I sent on your V-mail, so she knows the latest news.

We still go on with our work here at home, although we don't have much heart in our job. There has been no word from Bill as yet, and he is always on our minds. At least we know where you are: safe. It would be just as bad for me if I did not hear from you. So please keep the letters coming as often as you can write. This not hearing and not knowing you and Bill are safe is hell....

With the intensity of the war against Japan increasing day by day, the news from there grows more and more. Yet I feel the struggle will be a long one and the losses on both sides will be tremendous. Know that my thoughts are with you all the time, praying that you will come home soon. Keep on being happy and write whenever you can. Love from all hands. My deepest love to you.

   Punkin

May 15, 1945

Darling

   ... One thing I am doing these days is following very closely the broadcast from the San Francisco Conference, the establishment of the UN. And reading, too. For here is a tangible living force that is to shape our future lives and living. I have been much interested to hear Com. Stassen, who has reported several times on the issues being discussed. His talks have been very clarifying and informative. Your May issue of Fortune included a supplement about Dumbarton Oaks and San Francisco. It is an analysis of the proposals along with suggestions for the draft

of the Charter of the so-called World Security Organization to be the UN. It makes some clear sense out of the hodge-podge of the many reports in the papers.

◆ ⋯⋯⋯ ◆ ⋯⋯⋯ ◆

May 15, 1945

Dearest Beloved,

Oh, my wonderful darling—this letter should be written and tucked away for someday when we are together again. For tonight my heart is filled with such longing for you—so great is my loneliness. Foolish one that I am, I let myself in for this by seeing "Since You Went Away." Tonight, it now stabbed me so poignantly, for you are far away from me—so very far—and I want you close beside me—holding me in your arms and telling me you love me. Even now the tears come as I write this. But I must be the brave one, always loving my sweetheart and clinging to the hope that the job you have before you will be accomplished and soon you will return.

I was so happy and gay, for today brought three wonderful letters from you. All day long my heart was singing with joy. Such beautiful letters telling what I want to know, the little things that make up your days—the same loneliness that strikes at night—your hopes, your disappointments; all telling me of your love.

Your Punkin is sending my love to you.

◆ ⋯⋯⋯ ◆ ⋯⋯⋯ ◆

May 22, 1945

Dearest Wonder Poppa of Mine,

Oh, I am so happy that you have reached a spot where you now can begin to work and to be happy in your work.

While there is no mention yet as to what your duties will be, I know from your letters how happy you are to be away from the Replacement Pool. They were such hard and difficult days and I wanted so much to be with you to cheer you on.

But now you have come such a long way—I shudder to think of my Poppa flying the vast stretches of the Pacific and I hope you do not have to be assigned to a job where you'll have to do much flying. I want my Poppa down on the ground, where he can dive for a foxhole if the Japs come with the bombs. Dutch New Guinea. Golly, I was so scared when I looked at the map. I had an old one and much of the country and islands there still in Jap possession.

Somehow, even though we are apart, I am glad that my Poppa had to go. When I think of the man to whom you talked who had been over 40 months and is just coming back—I am happy in my heart that my Poppa is perhaps giving someone a chance to come to his home. We have had so very much that we must be happy despite this separation. If you were in that situation, we would not have had the lovely three years of being together. The time will go by quickly that you are in a job contributing to winning the war. Already, I can see the change in my Poppa.

Love,

Your Punkin

━━━━━━◆━━━━━━

May 24, 1945

My dearest one,

...But don't become downhearted, Darling, for I am writing to you every blessed minute that I get a chance to, and so you must know there is mail on the way. I got your three letters today. As I read and re-read them, I, too, experience the same

joy and discouragements my Poppa has gone through. How I wish I could have been by your side during those dark and dismal days. But you must not feel down in the dumps. You are my big strong Poppa who is a good soldier and who now has a job to do. Come on now—chin up—smile for me—you are my big strong, bravest one and I love you like sixty.

Love,

Punkin

◆ ⋯⋯⋯⋯ ◆ ⋯⋯⋯⋯ ◆

May 25, 1945

Darling,

How I miss you tonight. I want to crawl into our pretty bed and snuggle with my Poppa and make with the pretty love. My sleep is so restless—somehow, I miss the security and the calmness that come having you close beside me—and I pitch and toss as I have never done before. Perhaps, in time, I shall make the adjustment complete—who knows you might even seem like a stranger when you come home. No, I don't think it would ever come to that—in fact, I am sure we shall simply resume our living just as though we had never been parted.

Love,

Punkin

◆ ⋯⋯⋯⋯ ◆ ⋯⋯⋯⋯ ◆

May 28, 1945

My dearest Sweetheart,

I am blessed indeed with such a wonderful husband as you. You are my bravest one—writing such wonderful, heartwarming letters to your Punkin. Three came today—two in the morning mail and then another just before dinner this evening. The last one dated the 22nd and written from #920 (Manila).

You seem to move from one luxury to another. This time —an air mattress and a real indoor porcelain horse. Better watch out or you'll be getting soft again.

But I am happy to know you have such fine men to work with. I know you will learn much that will be invaluable. And they'll like my Poppa—never fear about that. Everyone likes my Poppa.

I do not like one bit that you must be a "traveling inspector." For it means, no doubt, you must fly. But I suppose I must get over that feeling because it ain't good. Everything is going to be OK. So, I mustn't worry.

I notice that there is "somewhere in the Pacific," so it looks like Poppa cannot tell me where he is.

Really and truly, I did not think you would be able to save any letters at all. Even mine because they do take up a lot of space. So do not feel you have to save them—as long as you are able to answer my questions. I shall save yours and one day we can open yours and you can tell me about them.

I never get started on your letters until late and now it's 1.30 a.m. But it is in the late hours of the evening that my loneliness is so great—that by writing you then, I can be so very close to you. You're my wonderful darling and I pray every night God is watching over you always and keeping you safe from all harm and danger. Be the happy one, my dear; I am always loving you and needing you so much. A big hug and a kiss and then just a whisper of a kiss as you go to sleep—a kiss which says, "I love the Poppa."

Always, your Punkin

CHAPTER 14

Dad Continues Flying the Pacific as an Army Air Corps Inspector

DAD WITH ONE OF HIS FAVORITES OFFICER FRIENDS, MAJOR BURFORD

DAD'S LETTERS (JUNE 1945)

◄ ·············◄············◆

June 12, 1945
Hollandia, Dutch New Guinea

Pretty Old Punkin of Mine,

Left the Philippines a month ago tomorrow, and tomor-row I go back for two or three weeks. Believe it or not, Manila is 1,925 miles from Hollandia. Distances here are the most amaz-ing things, particularly when the only practical way to travel is by air—you have no other basis of judgement, assessment than air travel. I can't say anything about mode of travel (kind of air-plane) except in the most general terms. Things that you can figure out by the aid of a map or atlas. Nothing specific as to routes, places, type of ship, conditioning, etc.

Just to give you an idea of what is happening in the Pacific Theater in the middle of June 1945, I enclose the front page of the World Observer, Armed Forces newsletter, printed in Manila at this time, June 14, 1945. In addition, American radio pro-grams are broadcast across these areas with news reports three times per day. Specific radio programs done in the United States are attempted to be played at their regular broadcast hours, Philippine time (9 a.m. East Coast / 9 a.m. Philippines; 13 hours ahead of the East Coast, but at times familiar to army and navy personnel.)

◄ ·············◄············◆

Thursday, June 14, 1945

My own darling,

Here I am, finally at the same HQ with the red marble floors I told you about. Back in the same region again I was in a month and two days ago. Suffice to say that the quarters and officers club here are in keeping with the red marble floor in the HQ building. We have a real Stateside porcelain horse—new toilet, an indoor shower in this annex to the club—right on the shore of the Manila Bay—a delightful situation. When I landed hot and dirty after many hours on route, I was ushered into the club bar and bought two highballs! Right over the bar! Delicious!

Have unpacked, showered, and had a dinner of Spam and mashed sweet potatoes and much good cold ice water. All served smartly by Filipino house boys. And now as I write with the beads of sweat falling from my brow, some delightful music is coming from the club. It's as clear as a bell and just loud enough to hear pleasantly. The point I started to make about the heat is that they're playing White Christmas!!!!

This place is much warmer than Hollandia and will be until November. But then they have a pretty winter season until May. I sure hope we won't be here to see another rainy season. As I said, I will be hopping about in this general vicinity interviewing various persons connected with the cases I've been assigned to investigate along with the stenographic work that has to be done to complete the reports. Probably here for two to three weeks.

Love,

D

◆┈┈┈┈┈┈┈◆┈┈┈┈┈┈┈◆

Fines haven, Australian New Guinea
June 15, 1945

My darling Jeanne,

Interviewed about three or four people. However, the main interviewees were gone from here so really, we came down on a wild goose chase. But it's one more station I'm familiar with, and it's a very comfortable kind of place. My quarters are comfortable, a whole hut to myself with plenty of space to myself. We are several yards back from the sea and at the back of the camp is the jungle—very beautiful to look at. The night noises are much the same as in the country at home—peepers and crickets and birds, etc. Had dinner with Lt. Bell and Capt. Temple, the two judge advocate boys I came down with. Had a "state-side" Coca-Cola, and then went for a pretty ride for an hour along the waterfront looking at the moonlight on the Pacific. This is the nearest I've been to the Punkin since April 15, 1945. Only 35 hours to 'Frisco.

I am so happy you're enjoying the sunshine and the beach in New London. You are lovely to my Momma and Poppa. They do enjoy so much you being with them. Mom's letters tell me what a wonderful one you are to be with them. Glad to hear about Jack's promotion.[8] I must write him, no doubt we'll be able to see each other in some bizarre place over here.

Love to Punkin,

D

----------◆----------

June 15, 1945
Somewhere in the Philippines

My Wonderful Punkin,

Off again in the morning for a series of short trips on my assigned tasks. Have to go out and rough it in the field. Going to be tough after the "fat-catting" around here. Just sent my laundry out to get my uniforms cleaned. It will cost me $6. So that gives you an idea of the inflation around here. So, you see things

---

8   Jack Fones, his first cousin whom he grew up with.

are going to be tough when we are permanently situated. But I shall continue to send home as much as I can each pay period.

Last night, I sat next to a major in the Corps of Engineers and had a Tom Collins! Struck up a casual conversation. I noticed from his broad R accent that he was from New England. I said, "You're from New England, aren't you?" Said he, "Yes from Connecticut." "Where?" said I. "From New London."" 'What's your name?" "Rob Potter." Well, we had quite a chat. He mentioned that he married John B. Bailey's daughter, of Bailey and Haub, an awning manufacturer. I said, "Which one? Pete or Edith?" He said, "Yes, Pete." Well, of course, you never knew many of my New London playmates, but Pete Bailey lived just up and across the street from us on Willetts Ave and in 1920–25, I used to play hide and go seek, football on what used to be open lots up along Ocean Ave. Major Potter and I had a grand chat about New London—mutual friends. Over dinner and afterwards, he had eight Tom Collins and I had four. But it was grand remembering about all those old places and faces. How we change. I wonder how I've changed so much from 1920. I mean complete changes of character, attitudes, and personality.

Love Punkin,

D

◆ ·············◆············· ◆

June 17, 1945
Somewhere in the Pacific

Dearly beloved,

This is the hottest place yet. I am wringing wet at 8 a.m. I don't know how one would actually work in this climate! I landed here yesterday after a long and arduous trip from dawn to 4 p.m. There is nothing so hot as an airplane on the ground in this climate and there's nothing so cold as an airplane at 7,000 feet with sweaty clothes on. On the ground they act as an oven. The aluminum body becomes intolerable as one taxies out for take-off. The doors are closed and the windows too. All the air that comes in leaks through the joints. Sometimes you have to wait for 15–20 minutes until you take off, and then in about 15 minutes you are freezing.

This installation is the most rugged one yet. However, the spirit is completely different from the Replacement Depot. Here in as much as you are a visitor of HQ, you are received with hospitality, courtesy, and for all the creature comforts that are available.

More later, Punkin.

Love,

D

June 18, 1945

Darling,

Having just met the husband of a childhood friend two nights ago, today I pitched in with a guy who was trying to unclog a drain outside our hut. We got talking and he said we had to create a dam like the one on Turtle Creek, PA. Turns out he remembers you and Bill growing up on Welsh Ave in Wilmerding. Earl J. Walker. Long story short, he had a book he was not reading and lent it to me, The Yankee From Olympus, a biography of Oliver Wendell Holmes.

As I was missing you tonight, I want to share a phrase from the book. Holmes is at home from the Army, recovering from his third wound in the Civil War. He is thinking of what he shall do when mustered out—talking with a friend about becoming a law student. Walking home afterward with John Ropes, "When the war is over," Holmes began. It was a refrain— enchanting, illusory as the 'Once Upon a Time' that begins all fairy tales. And how true that seemed tonight. Illusory as a fairy tale. I am committed to the end of hostilities, come what may. And how soon can we look for hostilities to cease? I keep telling myself that the end will come this autumn. But then I sneer at myself for wishful thinking. But it's nights like tonight I feel that you are particularly near, that even the thought of being away until autumn or January '46 is unbearable. Although I must admit the time is flying by and we all know by passage of enough time, the job will be done.

So, hurry and speed—O. Time in thy flight.
It's you that I need—Beside me tonight.
Love,
D

June 19, 1945

My darling,

Tonight, between dinner and the movies, we took a ride for an hour around the waterfront of this area. Very interesting. The native Filipino villages, however, are not picturesque or quaint. They only are dirty, untidy, and smell bad. The people here are considered different from those in Manila. The same as the people in NY differ from those hillbilly sections of our backwoods, only to a much greater degree. We also saw a Jap prison camp. They were remarkably healthy and well-fed looking. They dress only in a loin cloth. The streams and the ponds are posted with signs, blood fish—Keep Out!

I find that although this job could be a mean, nasty, and ill-tempered one, that being decent, shaking hands, being candid, smiling and being affable, and believing in the best of everyone, I have no trouble at all. They seem willing to believe that I am impartial, trying to establish facts and am going to present the reports in as fair and favorable light as possible. That's all for tonight.

Hugs and kisses,

D

--------------◆--------------

June 21, 1945

My precious Punkin—How disappointing. Back to the red-tiled floor HQ and no mail after a week. If I were to tell the truth, I came early just to see if there was mail. So, I decided to light out for civilization and this beautiful place with the indoor shower and the free-flowing porcelain horse and finish my reports here in surroundings so much more pleasing to my aesthetic soul.

Went to dinner at the Officers' Club—roast beef and two Tom Collins. It seemed just like the Lake Shore Hotel in Cleveland—Nautilus Room. It is right smack dab on the Bay. The sound of the waves is exactly like Lake Erie. Nothing like the ocean or Long Island Sound at New London. There the ocean waves are intermittently quiet and then they crash as they point up the beach. Here, as in Lake Erie, the waves are little, and their noise is continuous but mild and restrained. There's a wonderful breeze off the Bay tonight. And although one still perspires freely at 9 p.m., the breeze is so refreshing you don't mind it. There is a brilliant moon. This garden with the scent of the flowers, the moonlight, the lights out on the bay, and the soft accompaniment of the surf. The music on the PA system, the lights from club are much like a summer dance casino—all this rejuvenates my spent soul that should be crying out for beauty in the horrid place I was in. If it is beautiful around me, I can sit peacefully and think when evening comes. Tonight, as I finish this, I shall stroll out by the balustrade, drinking all this beauty deep within me as I quietly smoke and think how wonderful you are.

  Love you,

  D

June 22, 1945

Dearly beloved,

  A very few short days ago, I was down in the dumps. Tonight, I am as happy as a clam as I can be without my Punkin near me. But when my mood is this way—when I can wear a clean starched uniform for supper as I am now, when I can look about me and see a lovely garden, color, green grass, or the sunset in the bay. I can think of you and be stimulated to go on to do the job and I don't quake at the thought of being away even though I miss you. But with these things and with your letters, I can be brave.

  Love,

  D

June 24, 1945

My Darling Punkin,

  I have some regulations to study tonight on a new subject—this Readjustment Program, the points system for returning home or for discharge. I'm getting so many questions on it from enlisted men who learn I am an Inspector. And I haven't kept up with the development at all. Being as low as I am, I am personally completely uninterested. I have the magnificent total of 37 points—not even half of what are needed. No battle stars, only one-month foreign service, only 35 months' service in the States; no kids for which you get 12 points apiece. So, I washed my hands of the system in the very beginning and said, "The hell with it." The only way I'll get back to my Jeannie is to beat the Japs to pieces. So, as these War Department Readjustment Regulations and Far East Air Forces Regs were coming out, changing their minds from day-to-day, I chucked the lot in the file box with a scornful, "Phooey." But now it's become an important morale question in every GI's mind that's been over here two years or more. So, I must learn what it's all about. I shall write you a pretty letter this afternoon. I love my Punkin

> *Many, many hugs and kisses.*
>
> *D*

June 25, 1945

My Dearly Beloved,

Here I am again, out in the wilds. This is the roughest place yet. But what cordiality and thoughtfulness. This is a tactical unit and the difference between it and the service command units is extremely noticeable. I traveled all morning and got here in time for lunch. Completed one interview and examination of some records; have a man to see for half an hour and then back to where I was until this morning. Everyone was extremely cooperative here and so I'll finish two days' work by tomorrow noon. Tonight, I am actually the farthest I have ever been west of the Punkin! That's a scary thought.

I've been wondering today if you will box my ears for writing the kind of letter I did yesterday. Suffice it to say, it had the desired effect and today I am calm and cool and untroubled by the fever.

Love my Punkin.

D

MOM'S LETTERS (JUNE 1945)

June 7, 1945

Dearest Sweetheart,

Oh, my Darling, can you feel the awful fear that is clutching my heart, the sweat rolling off my brow, the sickening feeling in the pit of my tummy? I am trying so hard to be calm and brave. An announcement has just come over the radio of a plane crash in Dutch New Guinea, in a highly impenetrable valley called Shangri-La—21 dead and two soldiers and a WAC the sole survivors. This is what I dread the most about your assignment. You must fly—and yet always in my heart there lurks that fear of flying. I know you are all right, for I feel certain that we are so closely united in thought and spirit that I would know the instant anything was wrong with you. But the sudden fear that clutched one's heart when such news is flashed over the radio—it is hard to express the feeling. But I have tremendous faith in God that he is watching over you always and protecting you from danger.

Love,

Punkin

June 10, 1945

Darling,

How is your job going by now? With two such splendid men to work with, you must be getting settled down in the job. Outside of the work, I know it must be dull and lonesome, but I am counting on my Poppa to come through with flying colors because he's that kind of a guy.

Now, we in the States are faced with a new Japanese threat. Suicide squad of piloted balloons with bombs. Already they have found one on the West Coast, balloons with bombs attached to them. Five casualties. From one in the interior of Oregon. What will they think of next? Maybe the concentrated B-29 raids on the Japan homelands will knock them out completely and they'll quit. How I hope so—because I want my Poppa and all the rest of the boys to come home.

Always,

Your Punkin

✦ ⋯⋯⋯⋯⋯ ➤ ⋯⋯⋯⋯⋯ ✦

Still in New London ..
June 12, 1945

Darling,

Just this minute, I have looked out the window to see the brilliant full moon—over my left shoulder. Maybe there will be a letter tomorrow. How I wish you were here tonight. It would be so pretty to walk with you, down along Pequot Ave and we could set on Mrs. Roger's private beach, huddled together. Together again—that seems to be the resounding theme all day long and all night too.

Love,

Punkin

June 15, 1945

Darling,

Here is a letter from Bill about the teaching job. "I have been going over the advantages and disadvantages of taking the teaching job. If I accept it, I would be given a definite assignment for quite a while. Probably more money and also no South Pacific for quite a while. On the other hand, I will be taken away from my outfit. In case this outfit goes home before going to the Pacific—I am just out of luck. Well, I told them I would accept it and see how things turn out. They are to let me know soon where I am going to be sent, so I'll let you know."

Now—what do you think of that! We are all being selfish, I know, in being glad of this assignment for Bill—we are a little sad to think that he will not be coming home on furlough. But it is such a wonderful break for him. We just can't have everything, and we should be thankful that he will be spared further fighting for a while. We are tremendously proud that he was selected—no doubt, he has been a good conscientious soldier and performed his duties in a manner that did call attention to him. I am pretty damn pleased with the Schubie-puss. It was a hard decision to make. How he has matured—he'll not come home the same Shubie he went out as....

Love,

Your Punkin

June 20, 1945

My dearest One,

So glad to hear that you have the possibility of transfer to the Inspector General's Department—to actually be an Inspector General. I can remember with what awe and respect the IGs were held when they came to make the annual inspections. Although you have not mentioned it, it was what you wanted. And I am so happy that this honor has come to my Poppa. You are so capable and well-equipped that I am not surprised to hear this. You will do it well. But then, you would do any assignment in the best manner possible.

Your reaction to the VE news—somehow, I felt you would feel that way, yet you were not "cheated." It was not as we thought it would be. Someplace, no doubt, there were gala celebrations— for the most part, there were mostly gatherings in the churches throughout this land. People were glad—there was a thankfulness reflected in their faces. But yet a determination that the war was not over—the Japs were still to be beaten and not until V-J Day would there really be a celebration.

We were glad it was over in Europe. We were glad that our Bill had come through safely this far. But our thoughts were— what next because he hasn't seen much action in Europe, he will be ones of those to go to the Pacific. And you, too, were in our thoughts—for you have just begun your tour of duty and it would be many months before the Japs would quit. Yet, what have we done. Bungling the job as usual. Good old Americans— they do it every time. And I feel it will be no different with the Japs. We cannot hope to beat them down as we did the Germans. It would take years to clean them out of the vast territory they now occupy. So, the best we can hope for is an unconditional surrender "with reservations." Maybe, by these terrific blows at the Jap mainland we can reach that day sooner, but there is no peace—no permanent peace in sight—not in our time.

Love,

Your Punkin

❖ ⋯⋯⋯⋯ ◆ ⋯⋯⋯⋯ ❖

June 22, 1945

Darling,

...Here in New London. Has Mom mentioned what a wonderful garden Neddie has this year? It is quite some project and he spends many hours on it. Squash, cucumbers, corn, tomatoes, beans, and so on. He was quite unhappy this evening, for Maud had to go to Boston today to the doctor because of an abscess on her hip. But we heard tonight that she was on her way home, so apparently it is nothing serious. I still haven't seen her since arriving, but I imagine she will be here tomorrow for dinner.

Speaking of dinner—lucky you—roast pork—hmm! We ain't seen pork for so long. Why don't you come home and fight the war like civilians? Tonight, we had creamed chip beef (meat?), last night's spaghetti—the night before, scrambled eggs.

Today, Admiral Nimitz announced the close of the Okinawa campaign. Now, where will the next blow be struck? How many more lives must be sacrificed before they will call it quits. And today the Queen Mary docked in NY with 14,526 returning veterans. It brought tears to the eyes to read about the return of these men and women. A brief respite—then on to more of the same cruel uncertainty. Celebrations continue for General "Ike" (Eisenhower). Never in the history of NY has one man been given such a return as he was. So, we go on, hoping and praying for a quick ending—so that you and millions of other Poppas can come home. And so, I go on loving you—so

*always dreaming of the day you will be back, of feeling you close
to me and whispering, "I love my Poppa."*

Always, your Punkin.

* * *

June 29, 1945

My lovely darling,

*First of all, now for a bill of health. Dr. Sulman called
this evening to give me the report. The reason for the listless and
tired out nervous condition is what you thought it might be a
long time ago. Under-active thyroid. The B.M. Test showed me
to be a -11, whereas the normal person's is a +3 or +4. Also, I
am the intoxicated one—nicotine intoxication—so it looks like
the momma must cut down tremendously the smoking and quit
eventually. That will be a difficult task because I like my cigarettes. However, it was reassuring to know that the chest x-ray
showed a clear lung and that the red bugs (blood cells) are only
slightly below normal. So, tomorrow, we start the business of taking more pills and start getting ready for making lots of babies
when the Poppa comes home.*

Love, P

* * *

June 30, 1945

My darling,

*Look here, my good and lawful husband, my benevolent
and generous provider. How long are you aimin' to stay overseas?
You say we should be saving for all these funds. I am not saying
we shouldn't help Momma and Poppa. But we are sending $50 a
month now. Ned is contributing too. But as long as Dad is working, we had better put the money aside to give to them at a date*

when he may not be working. And I don't feel the burden should be all ours. Even if Herb has his family and expenses, he should help, too. After all, he is settled whereas we have had to traipse all over the country for almost three years and when you come home, we want to settle down, too. I want to help Momma and Poppa all that we can without letting ourselves get into a hole.

Love, your Punkin

CHAPTER 15

Ned and Maud get married in New London as Mom orchestrates the Wedding

DAD'S LETTERS (JULY 1945)

July 5, 1945

Darling,

I am enraged. I am so blind mad that I even wrote on the pad cover of my stationery! Major Hillis has been breaking the rule for inspectors who are on the road for extended periods—that their mail can be put in official mail pouches to all these small island bases. I didn't know anything about this and thought it was regular practice. So this boorish bastard gets a hold of my note to Lt. McQuade and proceeds to chew my fanny out for trying to go over his head in running the office—for

135

giving illegal instructions and everything else, ending that he had given instructions to hold up my mail until I returned to the home base. Oh, I'm swearing and tearing my hair. Written three blistering letters but have torn them up. He's the assistant boss and holds the whip and can influence the efficiency rating. He can have me transferred to some god-awful job. Of course, he is guilty of a highly illegal action not forwarding my mail by Army Postal Service, beside it being unethical and childish. The hurt comes from the fact that it takes away the one thing in my present life that is absolutely essential.

Love,

D

July 11, 1945

Darling,

But the most important of all is the spirit with which everyone "takes care" of you. Seven hundred miles from any-thing is this tiny little spot and they make you feel right away as though you belonged, as they knew you, too, were fighting this war and that they were glad of your help—glad to share whatever they have to make your journey more comfortable.

I've been reading this book on Ben Franklin and I have been thinking about Philadelphia and Pop Sweeney and his note on orientation, etc. And along the lines we've been discussing about setting up our own shop. There's no need for a precipitous decision, but I've been thinking that it might be a better idea for us to have some kind of plan for after the war. Somehow, I have a vague feeling that we'd be more at ease if we had a tentative plan of action. I'd love to hear you discuss it when you are in the mood.

◆ ·············· ➤ ·············· ◆

July 12, 1945

Darling,

Went out on the boats, Army Air Corp ships in Manila Bay, again today. Col. Burford has turned up some pretty nasty problems of organization and administration, and asked me to help, which flattered me considerably. I believe I can be of considerable help to him. He is like our old friend Uncle Harold Pierce at the Penna. Economy League. He knows his stuff completely. He's a damn good inspector, but his grammar and syntax are something else and his ability to express what he finds runs into problems when he has a lengthy, complex, involute problem that must be compacted into four paragraphs of an IG. Action Letter.

Saw "The Corn is Green" with Bette Davis tonight. I am so fond of plays. The real theater, I mean. That's one side of my life that I've never had a chance to share with you. When we were first married, we were too poor—when we were in Kansas, there were no plays. But it's one thing I love deeply, going to the theater. We must go a lot when I come home. I like the intensity of the stage. The feeling of being a part of what's going on. Oh, I act out every scene with every player, each line is tasted as a rare morsel of delicate food is tasted. I am fond of musical shows and variety shows in big places. But for a genuine thrilling evening, I like better a good play in a small theater, like the Walnut in Philadelphia where you practically sit on the stage. A quiet, intense, appreciative audience, to play with emotion, plot, sadness, and joy, becoming manners, a restrained elegance in dress and stage decoration. Friendly players who make you feel as though you like to know them and spend time in their company. You know, I've only mentioned it in passing but I used to "be in" plays. So many. You ask my momma. She suffered me

137

through many of them. So, in my old fogie way I am a dilettante
of the drama. Good night, my darling.

   Love,

   D

◆┄┄┄┄┄◆┄┄┄┄┄◆

July 22, 1945

Darling,

   I had your lovely letters of July 12 and 13 this noon—such
excitement (wedding). I hope everything went nicely. I shall be
atwitter till I have your letters describing all the details. Back to
the wedding. I'm sad to hear that Mama didn't approve. That's
to be expected. Mamas never approve, I guess, even when ideal
conditions exist. I know you will be the pretty one and try to
help her see the light if she will let you. Just think if we'd met
when we were Ned's age. We'd have a dozen kids by now. So, the
Methodists won out again. So, fie on you—you are a prosely-
tizer! Had Maud given up the Catholic Church before this or was
it done at this time? And how about her family? Are they still of
the Catholic faith? How too bad that such things act as a hurdle.
Cousin Alma and Eddie have had the same problem. I hope the
two kids have talked it through, so they know where they stand.
As you know, you and I have learned the hard way, there is no
problem insoluble in marital relations if they are faced quietly,
calmly, and affectionately. I'm just wondering what I can tell
Mama to facilitate her understanding. I'm pretty sure once the
deed is done, she will change her viewpoint. It's not a question of
reasoning—I think—but rather a deep-seated inhibition against
change. You are the wonderful one to be the Poppa's represen-
tative in all. I want you to feel free to act for me in all arrange-
ments that come up. Because I know you will be the fair one to

all. I have the utmost confidence in your judgement. I don't want you to worry about the responsibility, but rather it gives you a chance to do something for me when I cannot be with my family. You will be tolerant of the "New England" attitude, I know.

 Love, D

July 29, 1945

 Darling, I am the saddest one today. In church during the service I had to fight to hold back tears somehow. I missed you so keenly. I envisioned being at church with you, in some beautiful state-side church on a sunshiny winter Sunday morning—clear, cold air, blue skies, pretty clothes. You have a fur coat and a fur trimmed hat. I was in a uniform, a nice new one—gloves and woolen service cap. We were clean and scrubbed. We went into the big church with the soft seats, heard the organ and the choir like the Tabernacle Choir in Salt Lake. And I was so close to you—we were holding hands and singing the hymns. Then you were not there, and I was in the jungles of New Guinea and so, so sad.

 The Punkin is sad, too. I can tell from your letters. New York wasn't as much fun for you as we hoped it would be. It's a horrible place when you're lonesome. I know, having spent two very lonesome years there working for Scovil. This business of being separated isn't getting any easier for us, is it? We thought maybe after a while we could get used to it. I know for myself and I gather from your letters that it gets worse. Longing for you

 Love,

 D

MOM'S LETTERS (JULY 1945)

◆ ·············· ◆ ··············· ◆

July 1, 1945

Dear Darling,

Last evening was so lonely. It seems sometimes like I just can't bear another minute away from you. Sitting alone on the porch, a beautiful star-studded sky—it was just too much. I try hard not to get that way, but one can't always stifle the loneliness and longing. I didn't write to you—just sat and looked at the skies, thinking of nothing, not even you nor how much I love you. Finally gave up and went to bed about 10.30 only to toss and turn in the bed. It was 94 in my little hot box.

I wish we knew where we were going to be after this is all over. Somehow, I don't think we have the spot yet where we will hang out hats. Berks County, PA, is the nicest place yet, but there is no future for the Poppa there, so it is out. When you come home, I hope we can afford the money and the time to go to the West Coast. I would like to see southern California and Washington and Oregon. Perhaps there is a little niche out there for us. What do you think? Or are you still too intimately linked with New England to break away?

Love,

Your Punkin

◆ ·············· ◆ ··············· ◆

July 10, 1945

Darling,

Do not be unhappy, my love—yours is the tremendously important job in helping to win this war. As you keep going back to these places, the folks will remember you as the good, understanding, likable inspector, and you will have many friends for you. You are the super traveling salesman now but working with a good product—the human element, not those old brass gadgets you used to peddle.

Your Punkin

———————◆————◆———————

July 12, 1945

My dearly beloved,

This—our day—has been such a splendid one. We got the nicest anniversary gift of all—Maud and Ned's announcement that they had decided to be married! This coming Monday, July 16. All the usual necessary preparations—blood test, procurement of license, purchase of rings—have been done. This evening, they are off to see the marrying man. You can't know how glad I am to be able to write this to you, and I know your blessings will be with them, too.

The only cloud that mars the happiness of this news is your Mama's unspoken disapproval. How I wish you could be here to talk to her. I have tried to, but she just won't listen. And she is a bit angry with me, as she feels I have done my share in urging them to be married. I have encouraged them to follow their hearts.

Love you,

Punkin

———————◆————◆———————

June 13, 1945

Such a busy day. Jane, Maud's older sister, and I were appointed joint chiefs of staff to supervise the coming nuptials. Today was spent in combing Connecticut for a dress for the bride.

The poor prospective bridegroom being chauffeur and waiting at the doorways of the hundreds of shops we entered and exited— to no avail. Finally, after so many hours we compromised and decided upon making the wedding dress ourselves—Jane and I will be there with thimble, thread, and needle.

Even had a job of finding a "marrying" man. The monsignor refused to marry them. Maud has been excommunicated from the church. The Baptist minister is on vacation. So, I am laughing with glee. You who were always sticking up the nose at the Methodists, it's to be a Methodist minister, a Mr. Bell in the Methodist Church. The reception will be a dinner at the Howard Johnson's. Herb will be best man. How I wish you were to be here—Ned does too. And the cake—to be a huge three-tiered one to come from the USCG training station at Avery Point.

Love,

Your Punkin

◆ ⋯⋯⋯⋯ ◆ ⋯⋯⋯⋯ ◆

July 15, 1945

My Darling,

Wow! I am beginning to think it's a darn sight easier to get married than to help someone else get married. Worn to a frazzle. But the wedding gown is finished! Including a little Dutch cap. Maud and Ned are so pleased.

Your Punkin

MAUD AND NED'S WEDDING PICTURE – JULY 16, 1945

July 16, 1945

My own darling,

Where to begin to tell you of this day. Jane and I performed and executed a masterpiece in administration. From 10 a.m. to 4 p.m., we were on the go. But at 4 p.m. and the wedding march pealed forth on the organ, Maud walked serenely down the aisle to join hands with Ned and be wed. How much like the staging of a theatrical production. But how busy the day—picking up the booze, flowers to be cut in Aunty Laura Greene's garden, going to the church to arrange the flowers on the altar, transporting the wine, glasses, and cake to the Howard Johnson's, picking up the corsages, last-minute touches on the gown, finding someone to give the bride away, all was in our hands.

Maud looked very, very pretty in her white lace gown; her sister Doris, in a pretty gown of blue net; Ned in his whites; and Herbie in a nice gray suit. A simple yet reverent ceremony made all the more impressive by the sincere friendly manner of the Reverend Mr. Bell. Then on to the Howard Johnson's for a fried chicken dinner. Lovely toasts including one to Momma and Poppa by Ned for their 39th wedding anniversary, which, as you know, is July 16.

Then on to the Sullivan's for some light refreshments.

How I thought of you all day long but especially when the vows were said, just as we did five years and four days ago!

Love,

Your Punkin

DAD'S LETTERS (JULY 1945)

―――――•••••••••••――――•••••••••••―――

July 20, 1945

My own darling,

Seeing people with babies has made me wonder: Will we be the same? Will our first thought always be the baby? Won't we go on enjoying the things we did before the baby—will we tie ourselves down to the baby? I have seen so many girls transfer too much of their thought and attention to the baby—I don't want to be like that—always, you are the first in my thoughts—I want to keep it the way.

Love,

Punkin

―――――•••••••••••――――•••••••••••―――

July 22, 1945

Dearest Darling,

After reading Dr. Sweeney's letter and listening to your thoughts, it seems like Philadelphia would be the logical place. Most of our friends are in the vicinity. I have sorority and college friends with whom I could renew my friendships. But most important, your pre-war contacts are there. I cannot completely reconcile myself to living in suburban Philadelphia but like all the rest of the people in the world, we must live where the bread and butter will come from. It still does not deter my hope that we can investigate the possibilities of the West Coast. The quest for good government is all over the country, and I think that there will a gradual shift of the center of all activities to the West. There may be a golden opportunity awaiting us in the West. To my mind, the East Coast will not play a major part in the post-war period. It is too set to go along as in the past—fuzzy and moldy in spirit. I like to think in my own mind that we are moving to another 1849 Gold Rush, that this time, a hundred years later, new and important discoveries, new problems will radiate from the Far West. Maybe a few years back east to get settled. What do you think, my Poppa? You are the one that always says, we must always go forward to new and better things. Love, Punkin

CHAPTER 16

The Americans drop the atomic bomb and the Japanese make their offer to surrender

(AUGUST 1945)

SINCE AUGUST 1945 MARKS SIGNIFICANT EVENTS IN THE WAR that Mom seems to hear about before Dad, I have chosen to put her letters first. Each of them had very different reactions to the use of the atomic bombs used on Japan. They eventually come to some middle ground. Their excitement that the war is almost over is palpable in their letters to each other.

MOM'S LETTERS (AUGUST 1945)

August 1, 1945

This morning when I woke up, I laid abed for a while—thinking and dreaming of my Poppa—reminiscing of this time five years ago after we got married. Remembering our weekends together—one in Harrisburg—the next one in Reading—the funny hot box of an apartment on Fifth Street with the birdcage on the stairs. What a hot depressing box it was and then the Poppa found the pretty little cottage in the country. How well I remember that weekend—my coming to Wernersville on the bus—we had a funny old high ceiling room in the hotel across from the station. I guess maybe we got something to eat and then we went out to the farm to visit with the Moore's to see if they would like us and if we would like them and the little house. I can't remember how we got our stove, but we had a stove and a house, and we were so happy and so much in love—with no money—just a gas range to keep us warn. How the Poppa did talk to me to sell me on the idea of the little house that weekend. And so, on Sunday, we went out to tell the people we would live in the little house in the country. That was when we came to New London and got Herbie's car and loaded it down with things from Hartford and NL and Ned drove back with us. Poor ole Ned sure worked that week—driving back and forth between Reading and Harrisburg. What a bare little house it was. My poppa writing the pretty letters during the week when he was all alone. Then the weekends with so much to do—cooking, washing clothes, to make a home for Poppa. It wasn't long before I came to live for good with my Poppa. At first it was such an adventure to be getting up before dawn, you are getting my breakfast, and off for the auto trip each morning and coming home to you each night. But as the weeks grew into months and it got colder, how I hated to get out of our nice, warm bed.

The tears came today when I remembered the big doggie. How you came to meet me that night, so I would not be afraid of the big dog chained in the garage. How he howled and ran up and down the cellar steps all night long and I was so cross with him because I didn't get much sleep. How lonesome and unhappy he was. How we finally decided to let him come live with us and he became our doggie and we loved him so much. Big ole lummox seemed so big he nearly broke your foot when he stepped on it. Someday, I hope we can find another big doggie like him—but I don't think there will ever be a time when the tears will not come from thinking about him.

Joy and sadness have been a part of our life and I know my sweetheart will feel as I do—each memory that comes to mind, whether happy or sad, only further increased the bond between us. We have shared much—we have much more to share.

Love to you,
Your Punkin

* * *

August 7, 1945

My dearest Beloved,

Please, my darling, do not think I am nagging you when I urge you to write to Bill. You know yourself how wonderful it is to get mail when you are so far off from all of us. Bill has learned the hard way about the bonds of friendship, the goodness of having someone interested in you, and what strength and warmth can come into one's life when one is loved. No, I am not asking you to love him as your own brother. But I know

Bill—I know that hard, cold indifference of his is only a cover as it was with me. All through our childhood and adolescence, we experienced the tensions and unhappiness of our family.[9] It resulted in misunderstanding, unwillingness to find the truth of our troubles, and, consequently, we built up a cold front—a hard shell, so to speak. Inwardly, I craved to love and be loved. And it wasn't until I met you and married you that I found happiness. If sometimes, it may seem to you I am overly filled with love and affection, it's because for so long a period it was suppressed and when release came, I just poured out all that was in my heart. Shubie, my brother Bill, is the same way and in every way I can, I want and try to help him. He hasn't yet found the one person in his life, like I have. If he learns before that time, it will be much easier for him. I know how I feel about Ned—he's not just my brother-in-law, he's a kid brother to me. Because I've come to know him these weeks I've been here, and I want to help him the way I do with Shubie.

August 6, 1945: The United States drops the first atomic bomb on Hiroshima, killing thousands of people and obliterating the city.

August 8, 1945

The news today is what everyone has been waiting for. And way over where you are, I bet the men cried out long and loud in applause. Russia declares war on Japan. I just happened to have the radio on this afternoon when the news first broke. When we think of what it means—shortening the war and

---

9   It is not clear whether Mom is referring to her dad's gambling problem or the resulting poverty and anger facing the family.

reducing the loss of life of our boys—it just can't be possible that the Japs won't surrender now. Funny how this news was able to make me feel glad, and yet the stories on the use of the atomic bomb nearly made me a screaming meenie. I still am trying to analyze why the thing affected me so. But not getting very far.

Oh, my dearest one, is it too much to wish that you might be home for Christmas? Just think what that would mean. I am the craziest one, ain't I? Here I go like the war was going to end tomorrow. Who knows—maybe it will—but probably not? It can't be far off.

How I hope and pray that this mess will be over soon. Then you can come home, and we can get our fingers into the biggest thing all—maintaining and really keeping the peace. It's gonna be a hard time to get along the next five or 10 years, but we'll see it through and be so very happy. Sweet dreams.

Punkin

August 8, 1945: The United States drops a second atomic bomb on the Japanese City of Nagasaki.

August 10, 1945, 9 am

Darling, oh my darling,

I don't know where to begin. We are all in a whirl ever since the first bit of news of the peace feeler from Japan has come over the radio. I am so shaken—I cannot keep the tears from coming—it is only that—if the war ends now in a matter of a few hours or days.

9:45 a.m.—a bulletin just came in. Secretary Forrestal hopes to have something definite on the surrender within 25 minutes. Back again—even if it is over, I am not happy only because it means my Poppa will soon be home, but because it also means no more sacrifice of human beings—soldier or civilian.

How I have tortured myself mentally—on what we have done. This atomic bomb—yes, it still bothers me. But maybe if the war is ended by its use, it will have been a good thing. Maybe it was God's intention to give us this way to stop war.

Really, I can't even write. I don't know what I am saying. I am all keyed up, waiting to hear if the news is really true.

But all this is insignificant. History is moving so fast today. We are all in a big production—the biggest I have ever experienced.

Love,

Your Punkin

⋆ ⋯⋯⋯ ◆ ⋯⋯⋯ ⋆

August 10, 1945, 9 pm

My dearest Sweetheart,

This has been a difficult day, a day of waiting, listening, and hoping. A day of praying that the enemy is offering to surrender completely and in good faith—that we as the Allies will accept this surrender. We have been glued to the radio, all day long.

The people are not jubilant—they are tense, the first impact of the offer of surrender left them breathless with its suddenness, but now they are grim, determined, and analytical. Too much has been happening this week: the bombings, Russia's entry into the Pacific war, and now the Japanese offer of surrender. How can the human mind stand up against such swift developments? What will be the result if peace does not come within the next few hours or days?

Your Punkin

◆··········◆··········◆

August 11, 1945

My dearest Sweetheart,

    You must be breathlessly waiting as we are. Even if the war ends, it's going to be a hard winter, as I can see. If we thought the war years were hard, what of the ones ahead of us. There will be bread lines, I fear. It took us quite a while to get going: Conversion to war production. But jobs were plentiful. Now we shall have the opposite. Not only will our domestic problems be great, but we still have a Europe to care for. And what further problems we'll have in the Far East, we don't know. Besides world problems, we will have our own problems to deal with, finding a place to live, finding jobs.

    Love to you, sweetheart,
    Your Punkin

◆··········◆··········◆

August 14, 1945

    My Darling, it is over—isn't it? Even though no official word from the White House has come, there can't be any doubt but that it is true. It is true now my Poppa will be coming home. Home to me—oh sweetheart, how wonderful. Even though you may be away for a long time yet, the certainty of knowing I can look forward to a day now is so wonderful. But the others who have been away so long must come first. I do not mind that. We have been separated for such a little while in comparison and it is only fair that those with the longest service overseas come first.

    I am also so happy, too, for Shubie—it is one step nearer for Shubie to get well. Yes, Shubie is the sick one—a mental sickness—yesterday a letter came from him—he went to the hospital in Passau, taking tests and on his chart were the words Neuro Circulatory Aesthesia. You know what it means—nervous exhaustion. I do not worry about him, for I know he is healthy physically and can overcome this. Part of it may be what he has seen and experienced in combat contributed to this condition, but the main cause is his girlfriend. He is depressed and blue because she doesn't write him.

He doesn't realize himself what is wrong—he asks me what the diagnosis is. I hope that someone over there—a doctor or a chaplain—talks with him and he can get it off his chest.

Love, Punkin

August 14, 1945, 9 p.m.

Darling—Oh my sweetheart—it is over—over—war is done with—peace is here. I cannot help it, but the tears come rolling down the cheeks—such sweet release. No more slogging through the mud and rain, no more fear of not knowing when the end might come for some little boy like Ned or Shubie—no more heartaches and sorrow.

There are so many problems ahead, but now awhile we cannot think of them. It's time to give thanks to God for this miracle. Remember how you felt that morning you left Salt Lake— how you wished for a miracle to happen to end the war. That miracle has come. Oh, darling, I am so choked up with emotion—I feel so close to you right now—I know what is in your heart and mind if only I could really be at your side now. I have a feeling it will be a long time before you come home. I pray it will not be too long.

All my love, Your Punkin

GENERAL MACARTHUR COMMANDS JAPANESE TO THE PHILIPPINES TO
NEGOTIATE THEIR SURRENDER.

August 15, 1945

Dearest Pretty Poppa,

Today, the word is that the Army will release 3,000,000 within the next year—500,000 a month. And my poor Poppa will be in the tail end because he went over so late and the word is too that the boys in Europe will not go to the Far East to be part of the Occupation Army. That also means that Shubie will be home for good. My Momma called me this morning to tell me how happy she was that you would be coming home. She wanted you to know that she hoped that you would be home soon. All over the world, there must have been tremendous celebrations last night. But I couldn't celebrate that way. It was much better to sit by myself—thinking of you—thinking of so many men of ours in Japanese prison camps; what a wonderful world it must have been for them when they were released. I thought of all those homes where they lost loved ones. The sinking of the cruiser Indianapolis came to mind. I kept thinking how long it will take to clean all the Japs on the many islands and other places, who may not give up. I keep thinking what a hard winter it is going to be—some five million unemployed by December. What are we going to do with those people? What are we going to do for those men coming out of the service?

I am driving home on September 4. Maybe I should go via Philadelphia and start the ball rolling in the apartment or living quarters section of future plans. However, with gas rationing over, I can drive back a little later. Have you given any thought to setting up headquarters in Harrisburg? Pop Sweeney's contact no doubt will be in the state government—well, who knows maybe the way will open up for us without all this worry. I do love you so much. Oh, Sweetheart—hurry home—I need you.

Always, Punkin

◆ ⋯⋯⋯ ◆ ⋯⋯⋯ ◆

August 22, 1945

Dearest One,

We had some disquieting news from East Hartford today. The Friday after we were there, Herb got his notice with one month's pay. They had done away with the plant newspaper, so he was out of a job. From 22,500 personnel, they had cut down to 6,000. If this is what is going to happen all over the country, we are going to be in a sad situation. In Herb's situation, they have decided to keep him on to run the Bee Hive, the plant magazine, I believe. Well, I hope he manages to stay on—it would sure be a tough break to be out of a job like so many thousands are today. Especially since they just bought the house and another baby on the way. I just got a call from my momma. Shubie is in England for the instructor's job for training the army of occupation. He almost did not get it because he had just gotten back from the hospital in Passau when he was called to the telephone. He will be living on a base—it's 12 miles from Blackpool—north of Liverpool. Mother said his letter was wonderful in spirit. It's given him such a tremendous boost, and it's just what he needed to get him out of this black feeling and mood.

Mother and Dad were so buoyed up by the news. Dad kept butting in on the conversation, "What about Don? What do you hear from him? Send him our best." I was so glad to hear all that and the whole conversation gave me a lift too. For how long I have hoped that Mom and Dad could get together and work and live as team, and it begins to look as though they have put aside their differences. It is the first time Dad has ever evidenced an open interest in Bill or me.

We need to talk about our dreams and how we are going to reach them as well. When you want to talk about them, share some in a letter. I love you so much.

Your Punkin

◆ ··········· ◆ ··········· ◆

August 24, 1945

Dearest Beloved,

What a heavenly weekend. Having three letters from you always makes me brighter.

I know just what you meant about the news of the surrender—it was so long in coming through that its effect had worn off when the actual announcement was made. Yes—there was much jubilation in the cities. It was good to hear that you will apply for discharge on November 19 when you turn 38. We are at a crossroads where you must make a decision: to remain in the Army or go back to civilian life. Either way I shall be happy. But if you decide to return to civilian life, I would get out of the army as soon as possible because opportunities with Dr. Sweeney may go to others if you are not around. Hurry home, my sweetheart. I love you like the devil.

Your Punkin

DAD'S LETTERS (AUGUST 1945)

August 1, 1945

My Wonderful One,

Another pretty day gone by. Thirty-eight years ago, three-and-a-half months before the Papa was born (1907), an Aeronautical Section was set up in the Signal Corps. Two years later, they got their first "flying machine." So we had a formal retreat formation this evening at 5.30 p.m., not so pretty as the reviews we had in Garden City but always impressive, always the catch in the throat as a body of troops stands rigidly erect at the salute when the band plays the National Anthem and the colors hauled down. Whether it's in Guinea or Kansas. Tonight, as we gathered around the flagpole on the side of our mountain, we could look down into the valley and see the big lake and then away to the South, range after range of green jungled mountains, hundreds of miles deep into Guinea and at our backs the dark green 7,000 feet of Old Cyclops, dark and foreboding—always with hovering clouds. And the pretty waterfalls halfway up....

Love,

D

August 9, 1945

My Pretty Punkin,

...Of course, we have been thrilled by the news—the atom bomb and Russia's entry into the war. Everyone has revised his estimate of the war's end. Some even are saying it will be only a matter of days. Most everyone now feels like certainly no later than Christmas. How wonderful it would be to be headed homeward by the end of the year.

That's all for tonight. I love the prettiest old Punkin. Here's hoping and praying next week's news will be good and the Japs quit right now! So, I can come home to my darling.

D

◆············◆············◆

August 11, 1945

Darling,

Wow—what news—we heard it last night at 9.30 on the Far East Network! Everyone is in a storm of excitement this morning. The big bomb—Russia's entry—new location—now the end in sight. At least two months sooner than even the most optimistic dared to hope. Now it's really possible to hope and pray that your Poppa will home or at least started for home by Christmas.

Last night after the news was acknowledged by Washington, you should have heard our WAC Detachment. Such cheering and screaming. You never heard more noise even for Frank Sinatra. They kept it up for half an hour. The enlisted men took it with a grain of salt—being so used to Army disappointments. The officers, for the most part, contented themselves with discussions of what the United Nation would do. But you could see in the faces of the old timers—24 to even 43 months (one Major Westbrook who bunks across from me—executive officer in the General's office—he will complete 43 months today)! All these old-timers just relaxed as if someone snapped a taut string—you could see the reflection of San Francisco in their eyes. Those guys should go right now! Then maybe with replacements from the States those of us who have been over can get back by '46. But regardless of all that—the end is in sight. Now it's a question of horse-trading and diplomatic gab, instead of killing and getting killed.

I don't know how much work will get done today. It's quiet right now, but I'm afraid the exuberance will break out at the slightest urge of more good news, which is all right with me. See you soon.

Love,

D

◆·············◆·············◆

August 12, 1945

…Well, of course, we're all hanging on the news with bated breath. We heard of James Byrnes' reply to the Japanese last night around midnight (11 a.m. Saturday your time). And, of course, there is nothing to do but sit and wait to see what they say. But it looks encouraging. I'm sure it's only a matter of days right now that hostilities will cease before Labor Day. Maybe even tomorrow. Then we'll see what we shall see. It is now 10 p.m. Sunday (9 a.m. Sunday your time) and all we hear is that the world still waits Japan's reply. Such a dramatic moment in history! Well, maybe we'll know in the morning. I love you, my darling. I am so hungry for a letter. But I am so much hungrier for this to be all over and for me to be headed east to be with you,

to hold your hand. To make the love, to pick up the intricacies of our life again. God grant that it will be soon.

Always faithful and devoted Poppa.

◆ ⋯⋯⋯ ◆ ⋯⋯⋯ ◆

August 13, 1945

My precious darling,

Still no big news. I'm listening tonight right now to the 8 o'clock news. Says we might have some announcement by 10 our time tonight. Work was pretty desultory today—even the boss didn't have his heart in it. Everyone started off the day in good spirits, but as the heat came on, all slowed down impatiently waiting for what everyone wants to hear. Tonight's radio, Monday night, like Stateside, is extra good music and we've been listening to several fine programs. Major Welling across from me has a fine radio, so get all there is on the Far East Network.

...Now here it is, another day. Tuesday morning—7a.m., August 14. World War I started 31 years ago today. Maybe the two will be known as the "Thirty-one Years War" if armistice comes today. But it cannot because we certainly won't make any armistice until they've signed and even then—there is always the possibility of some hideous trick—they were bad ones in December 1941 when they talked peace and blew us all to Hell at the same time. So, you can be sure that whoever talks peace for our side is going to do it, this time down many gun barrels and under an airplane protection, I betcha. Must go to work.

Love,

D

◆ ⋯⋯⋯ ◆ ⋯⋯⋯ ◆

August 15, 1945

My Wonderful Punkin,

    Well, the news is in; but it leaves us all pretty cold. Somehow, we don't seem to be delirious and enthusiastic. Some of it is due to the way the news was so long and drawn out—but then most of it is due to the fact that Service Commands are disillusioned places anyway. The tremendous fact that the killing has stopped is, of course, lost on our people because except for very rare instances they have never been under fire. Then, too, ours is a colorless command, and all we do is work like in a factory or office—in fact, so far as we know yet, we don't even get a day off for any celebration—and we might even have to work Sunday as usual. All this plus the fact that our work will continue in reverse, hauling supplies, storing things, and generally straightening our supply and maintenance of Air Corps supplies and equipment. Sometimes, it seems like it would take 10 years. But I suppose things will get rolling after plans get made and decisions are ratified. But this thing came so suddenly that it caught us at full speed in high, in a forward direction and now we must stop, shift the gears, and throw the machinery in reverse. But any way, it's over and there is a new ray of hope in each person's heart that he or she will be among the first to get home. There is practically no celebration in the barracks tonight. One of my next-door bunk mates cracked a bottle Old Overholt. Four or five of us sat around drinking straight whiskey out of the bottle. The old timers shooting the breeze about how tough it was three years ago when the campaign was getting started. But no one even mildly approached getting high. I suppose downtown it's a madhouse. The radio tells us that all over the States, cities are wildly jubilant. I have the same feeling I did on VE Day, sort of left out of all the fun. The hopeful thing I can think of is that on November 18, I will be 38 and by then those over 38 or older may request relief from active duty. But for that possibility, I would be dejected indeed because there are so many who have been over here so much longer than I have.

I wish I could build up some enthusiasm about this cessation of hostilities, but I just can't seem to realize what it means to all of us. We folks over here and all the folks at home. All I can think of is home to you. Everything also is insignificant, and home seems so distant and intangible at this moment. When I get your letters next week about these days, I suppose I'll enthuse and feel what it means to me. Now, I am going to bed to dream of you.

Love,

D

August 18, 1945

My Own Punkin,

...Our work still goes on, as usual. One change. We have Sundays off; at least, we have tomorrow off. There has been a dislocation in the mail service what with all the excitement and we hear that we'll not have any mail at all for five days. Also, we may not be getting our mail out as promptly as before, so there may be a break in your receiving them. There is much uncertainty in the air. No decisions can be made until we get the Nips signed on the dotted line and neutralize their arms and facilities. It may take a couple of weeks. So, I assume the immediate future will continue to be highly uncertain. All the high point men (for discharge) and the enlisted men over 38 have their one foot practically on the boat and their bags packed, hoping they'll be home before the end of September. Those of us who are low-point men look upon them with envy and scorn and heap abuse upon them

at the slightest provocation—all in fun, of course. At the present moment, I have only 37 points, but I may have five more by virtue of a campaign star on my Asiatic Pacific Ribbon for which I was lying on my bunk in the Replacement Depot. That would give me 42 points up to May 12.

By the way, discount all this malarkey about the Army point system being the choice of the GIs. I have not heard one person, officer, or enlisted man, say he thinks it fair. The tremendous weight given for kids, 12 points each, up to 26, is of course horribly unfair to people like you and me. The very minor credit given for overseas service is unfair. Many boys have been away for over 30 months and still do not qualify for the critical score of 85. And, of course, the battle star credit of five points is a plain racket. Everyone agrees the combat soldiers who were shot at and risked their lives time and time again deserve extra points, but the battle stars on the theater ribbon is not a satisfactory determination. So, when you hear anyone say it's the GI's own system, tell them for me to go to Hell because the GIs in this theater are vehemently against it. It may have been fair in the European theater, but it just doesn't work over here. The sooner the War Dept. realizes it, the better morale will be....

Love,

D

August 19, 1945

My dearly beloved,

...Well, I hear our little friends (the Japanese commanders) came in today. They landed about three miles from where I'm located. But the field was closed. Some of the pilots in my barracks had business there, though, and saw the whole

business. They said they were cocky little devils, strutting from the plane to car, all dressed up with gold braid, insignia, and medals. They were received with full military courtesy and formality. When you think of what happened at Corregidor and the "Death March" from Bataan, it sure makes one want to skin them alive. But it will save many, many lives to accept this way instead of having to make an invasion, and if MacArthur runs true to form, he'll crack down on them once he has the signed paper in his bank.

Of course, like everyone else in the States, according to the radio, we have in the back of our heads, that possibility that may be a prelude to some gigantic deception. But if it is, the furies that have gone before will be as calm as a zephyr compared to the onslaught that would any treachery. Because every last American serviceman is in no mood to fool around. They want to go home. They've been away too long, and they're fed up with the whole business. So, if things go right, each one will take it as a personal gyp on the part of the Nips and they'll blast the islands right dab out of the Pacific Ocean.

August 22, 1945

Darling,

...I am considerably surprised—I guess no, not surprised—concerned or intrigued or something about your reaction to the atomic bomb. That is what war is. Destruction. That's all it is—destruction of the enemy, his people, his equipment, his land, his ability to live, and, above all, destruction of his will to fight. In modern war, there is no plan to stop short of the absolute. There are no halfway stand-offs. Either he destroys you, or you destroy him. It is the military commander's duty to use every

resource he can command to attain that end—no thought can be given to humanity, to making it easier on the enemy. The sole objective is to destroy more of him than he can destroy of you. Therefore, any means can be and must be justified if the cause of the war is justified. I personally believe we would have used gas if we thought the result would give us a definite advantage. And so, would the enemy, if he thought it would have been to his benefit. Thus, the means or measures of waging war cannot be judged by any concept at all except the ultimate result. It is the one case where the end does justify the means. That is why the most awful fact is the actual going to war. The time to be horrified and prayerful is at the moment of going to war. Once the blow is struck, once the die is cast, there is nothing else to do but hit with everything you've got continuously and without surcease as long as the enemy has left to fight with or until he is ready to quit. It is a certainty that if Germany or Japan had discovered this device first, they would have used it on us—that, however, is not the prime argument. The fundamental point is that war knows no degree. It has no rules or ethics—no law— and that is what makes it the horrible thing it is. So much for the old bomb.

◄┄┄┄┄┄┄◆┄┄┄┄┄┄►

August 23, 1945

My Darling,

 My next-door neighbor handed over his August 20 issue of Time. So, I had to read all the articles about the atomic bomb and radar. I begin to see how you were upset by the atomic bomb. The Stateside stories were far more awesome than they fed to us. It is a frightful thing, surely.

...Well the radio tells us that the air echelon will move into Tokyo on Sunday and the water echelon two days later. And the papers to be signed a week from tomorrow. I feel sure all will go well. The few families will be given short shrift and instead of losing thousands of lives and other casualties. The Japs can do nothing else because they are surrendering all over the place: China, Guinea, and here on Luzon. And they admitted they had no Navy left nor gasoline for their planes. So, they will have to give up.

◆ ············· ◆ ············· ◆

August 24, 1945

What's this about ole Shubie? He's the last guy in the world I'd figure for the heebie jeebies (emotional illness). He always seems so able to absorb troubles and stuff. Maybe his sudden transition from boy to a man. Like my reaction to the transition from a peddler to student. Ask Alma what a wreck I was over Christmas vacation 1938. I'm sure Shubie will shake this business off with some rest and stability. I hope he can forget this biddy who has got in his hair. Those things are tough. Even I can remember the pangs of unrequited love. Oh, how I suffered. I hope he doesn't fall for her again when he gets back home....

Love,

D

◆ ············· ◆ ············· ◆

August 27, 1945

Darling,

In Abbie's letter was a picture of the wedding. Ned and Maud coming out of the church, and there's my old Punkin with a smile four miles wide and such long hair. You'd mentioned it but hadn't realized the difference. Ned and Maud look so happy. You did a wonderful job on Maud's dress. Even the flying rice shows up in the picture.

Your philosophy: bright, gay, glamorous, exciting, incurably romantic spark zest and joy. Warm meaningful hugs and kisses, gladness, spontaneous enchantment—lifelong honeymoon. Those are the words—that is the philosophy we will live by. All the years of my youth I was groping in vain for just that and I had about given up and was letting my cigar ashes fall on my vest when you came by. I was worried sometimes during the "hard" years because life had ground us down and seem to be bending us to a wheel. You had erected a shell about you in defense against the ills and evils in the world, and I couldn't get through it. But, then, as the years ran by, we cast off our cocoons and came out dancing in the buttercups in the moonlight. I can't imagine anything more ecstatic than "growing old" with you.

August 29, 1945

Darling,

Your thinking about the way you want to live pleases me. When you have achieved those attitudes, you are the true philosopher.

It's a hard decision to make whether to take the broad highway of adventure and go chasing stars sliding down the moon beams, soaring on rockets or whether to take the well-travelled country lane and settle forever in one community and grow out our lives in one place. Maybe we're too old now to become the settled ones. Maybe the Army and our schooling has given us a bad case of wanderlust. All I know is that if I have you by the hand and enough to feed and clothe us, I don't care much which road we follow or where it takes us. Just you and a place to make the babies, that's all I ask. Keep after that paintbrush and give it the devil. Every day I love you more and more. Good night to the pretty Punkin

CHAPTER 17

War Ends in the Pacific, Dad off to Brisbane on an Inspection

MOM'S LETTERS (SEPTEMBER 1945)

◆ ⋯⋯⋯ ◆ ⋯⋯⋯ ◆

September 2, 1945: The Japanese officially surrender in Manila, in the Philippines.

◆ ⋯⋯⋯ ◆ ⋯⋯⋯ ◆

AFTER THE DRAMA AND EXCITEMENT OF AUGUST WITH news of the atomic bombs on Hiroshima and Nagasaki, Russia's entry into the war against Japan, Japan's peace feelers to the Allies, and the negotiations for the unconditional surrender, Mom and Dad report to each other on how they learn about the final surrender in Manila on September 2, 1945. Although every letter talks of when Dad might be home, dates vary wildly from Christmas 1945 to December 1946. Soon, however, Dad becomes focused on a two-week inspection trip to Australia with one of his favorite commanding officers, Lt. Colonel George Glober.

September 1, 1945
Hotel Chatham
New York, New York

Darling,

There just wasn't enough time for doing everything. I went shopping for clothes for the first time since you have gone away. I finally succumbed to the desires for something new. No—it's not a fur coat, but it was a pretty chocolate brown gabardine suit, which I know you will like so well.

After a short rest and shower, we hopped a cab for Dot and Dick's. Nice talking, drinking Old Fashioneds, and then a delightful supper. After that, a walk along the river and then back to listen to the broadcast of the signing of the surrender. Dot drove us back to the hotel, where we have been packing for the train to NL tomorrow a.m. Need to sleep. Hurry home, my darling. How I miss you and need you.

Your Punkin

Mother brought this letter from Bill who has started teaching at an armed forces school near Blackpool, England.

"Dearest Mother,

Here I am in England and what a set-up, formerly used by the Air Corps. I am going to be an instructor in the milling machine section. A lot of the instructors are civilians from the States. The school will be open for a year. We have great living facilities and are right near the bus stations, which takes us into the surrounding towns. Blackpool is the summer and winter resort for England, and it is only eight miles away. They have everything there; I go dancing almost every night. We are finished by 5 and have weekends free. We have an ideal set-up here and to think the Air Corps had all this while we were out there fighting and living in fox holes. They don't know how lucky they were. How are you and Dad doing? Is Jeanne home yet from New London? Take care, and I will write after school starts. Love, Bill."

He's gotten such a wonderful break this time. And no signs now of any neurasthenia (nervous exhaustion).

Love from your Punkin

◆··············◆··············◆

This is Mom's last letter that was saved. There is reference in another of Dad's letters that he has packed up over 200 of Mom's letters and shipped them home in a box with some other important items. We found a couple of first pages of letters #199 and #200, so we are sure she kept on writing him. As bases were being decommissioned, there was little space to store things either in his office or in the barracks, as the guys were constantly being moved.

DAD'S LETTERS (SEPTEMBER 1945)

◆··············◆··············◆

THE END OF THE WAR DOES NOT BRING THE ELATION THAT Dad expected. He knows he has six more months to live in this tropical climate, with no real mission to perform and he wants to be home with his Punkin. He is looking forward to an Inspection Trip to Brisbane, Australia, with his good friend Colonel Glober, which keeps him excited and active for much of the month.

◆··············◆··············◆

September 2, 1945

My dearly beloved,

The Day! Six years less one day since I sat in Mrs. Flanagan's boarding house in Harrisburg at 5.30 a.m. and heard Mr. Chamberlain say, "We are now at war with Germany." And I was falling in love with you. There were tears because I felt we would be at war in a matter of months and all thoughts of love and marriage to my Punkin would be swallowed in the swift turn of events. But it was not to be. We must always thank God or Fate or Fortune that sufficient time was granted to us not only to formalize our love but to live together these glorious five-and-a-half years and weld our lives into one life together, unshakable and everlasting. What six years it has been! What a metamorphosis has the world undergone. And our lives and personalities with it. In but a moment the first shortwave broadcasts will start to come in from Tokyo that the old era is over. That the brave, new world has begun. What a wonderful thing it will be for us— the Punkin and the Poppa—to join hands forever and take our place in some small way to bring peace to our world. We heard the description of the signing—Mr. President and Gen Mac, and Admiral Nimitz. It was very moving. We were gathered around Welling's radio, and both Westbrook and I broke out a bottle of whiskey. So, we poured drinks of straight whiskey all around for about five of us and waited until MacArthur signed. As the broadcaster spelled out D-o-u-g-l-a-s, we struck glasses and it was over.

Love,

D

September 4, 1945

My darling Punkin,

Busy most of the day. Things are getting busier now with the shock of the end of the war over. People are swinging into action—after sitting around in a trance for two or three weeks. The shock of some and the sensing excitement dislocated all divisions. But now the ordinary flow of paperwork starts again— just like war time. And, of course, the service offices, such as inspection, personnel, adjustment general, judge advocate, etc., are busier than ever while the direct labor people, such as supply and maintenance, are tapering off. And, of course, as they can turn lose their people, the aforementioned services units can begin to cut down. So, it's just like Garden City, but in reverse.

* * *

September 8, 1945

Darling,

I have been thinking a very great deal about staying in the Regular Army—but I am still undecided—the main reason being that if I make any definite commitment, it will surely tend to keep me over here longer, I'm afraid, or it would mean returning overseas after a short stay at home, which is out for my money.

So, I'm just coasting along, doing my job—take on added responsibilities because I'll no doubt be left with the regulars to break in the new volunteers, who we believe will be coming over the first of the year. But when I finally become eligible, I'll be in a positive mood to choose. So far, however, I am no further ahead in my thinking. The way it looks now I should get home sometime between April '46 and July '46. What do you think? Should we stay in the Army? You haven't said, but I think you want to.

Please tell me if you can. It will mean traveling around and no pretty little house for several years. But maybe it would mean a better house when the time came. Tell me what you think—forgetting, if you can, the question of how it would affect my getting home. Glober, my friend and CO, has been talking me into staying. If all the colonels and Lt. Colonels were like Col. Maugham and Glober, I'd stay in a minute.

    Hugs and kisses, Punkin

    Love,

    D

◆ ⋯⋯⋯ ◆ ⋯⋯⋯ ◆

September 9, 1945

Darling,

    Received instructions from the Colonel to be ready to leave for Australia on Monday morning prepared to make inspections of Purchasing and Contracting Office in Brisbane, Australia. It's early spring there, so I need to take my wool uniforms and will be chilly in the evening. We also may make some inspections of bases that are closing up. Because I'll be with the colonel, don't worry. He is a good flyer. Lt. Col Glober will be his co-pilot—so we are good.

    Love,

    D

◆ ⋯⋯⋯ ◆ ⋯⋯⋯ ◆

September 16, 1945

My dearly beloved,

    I've never loved you or missed you more than I do right now. Ever since I hit civilization again, the loss of you has been stabbing me at every turn, every minute, every incident. A new city, Brisbane, with all its discoveries to be made. Stores, public buildings, streets, people, trains, parks, and everywhere I look and go, my hand is empty of yours and there's no little one skipping by my side to see with me. I feel bad enough—so I'll not make it worse by dwelling on it.

Upon landing, the girl driver drove us up to a hotel that is for Colonels and Lt. Colonels. While my two carmates, argued about whether they would share a double room, I picked up my luggage from the car and walked off and left them arguing. Have not seen them since. But what fun I've been having all by myself. A lovely hotel room. Two big soft beds, a wonderful shower/tub, all the rest of it. Pretty towels and an easy chair, bureau, and writing desk. This will be great staying here. I just had a great meal of fresh fish.

Love,

D

◆ ⋯⋯⋯⋯ ◆ ⋯⋯⋯⋯ ◆

This trip seems to bring Dad and Lt. Colonel Gober closer together as friends, really the first person Dad has become friends with overseas.

◆ ⋯⋯⋯⋯ ◆ ⋯⋯⋯⋯ ◆

September 21, 1945

My Dearly Beloved,

...Lt. Colonel Glober and I were going to a variety show tonight, but at dinner he began feeling ill and excused himself— asked me to take care of the check—and went up to his room. I haven't gone to check, but I am little worried about him. Ever since he came over to Manila, he's been feeling lousy. Manila's climate got him down, as it does all of us. But when he landed

here, he seemed to regain his zest as we all did. This is the most beautiful climate right now I've ever seen. Anywhere.

Glober's about 6'4" and probably doesn't weigh 150 lbs. He's a scrawny and thin and has no color at all. Chalky white. He has a wife and one-year old boy in Washington D.C. His father-in-law is a retired major general. He was a bomb group commander early in the war. Combat in the Solomon's, the Battle of Midway, and all that, way back in '42 and '43. Five medals for bravery, etc. He went to Command Staff and then the Naval War College and was shipped out to go on MacArthur's staff as an amphibious air planner. Somewhere along the line, his papers got tossed in the wrong basket, and he wound up in our Command. We have become friendly on this trip. Both of us are reserved and hesitant about making acquaintance, so we had hardly talked to each other in the office—our work being in entirely different lines, mine with investigation and his with technical inspection. But now, we have apparently fallen into a team. It looks as though after the smoke clears away and all the people get out that are going now, he will be head of the technical section, and I will be head of the administrative section. At least that's what he says, and he is now deputy to Colonel Maugham. Consequently, we have had many long talks here in Brisbane as to what is wrong with our inspection office. And we've agreed on policies correcting the wrongs to be mitigated as soon as we get back and all the old hands are cleared out.

His family lives in Georgetown in D.C.—a graduate of 39A flying school in the regular army and a senior pilot. One of the things that drew me to him was the other night we were drinking beer in his room. And some of the biddies called to ask us to some party. He came back from the phone and said, "I took the liberty of refusing for both of us." You know I'm not much of a rounder when I am away from home. So that made him pals with me then and there.

CHAPTER 18

With No Mission and Poor Health, Dad's Depression Deepens

DAD'S LETTERS (OCTOBER 1945)

—⋯⋯⋯⋯—⋯⋯⋯⋯—

October 5, 1945

Darling,

...Well, it's Major Donald E. Dunn, Inspector General Division, instead of the Air Corps. Yep, the news was waiting for me when I came back. Your fat old Papa is an Inspector General. The appointment was made by the War Department on September 19, 1945.

Love you, Punkin,

D

—⋯⋯⋯⋯—⋯⋯⋯⋯—

October 13, 1945

Darling,

    The Leyte inspection is over, and we return to Manila in the morning. It's been an unsatisfactory experience. No one cares anymore. The sole thing on everyone's mind is going home. Not only those we are inspecting, but ours too. It doesn't make sense to keep going through the motions of normal routine, but these places have got to be closed up. I sure don't know who's going to do it. The men just coming over are infected by the old-timers, and as a result, nobody does anything but sit around and count up points and swap the latest rumor about what ships are due when and when will they go out. Very disheartening. Every day, I want to get home more badly than the day before....

    Love,

    D

October 15, 1945

Darling,

    ...So, all the goof-offs get to go home and your Papa who does his job as good as he can—has to stay. But that's the way it should be. We'll get the job done much sooner and better. You remember how we used to talk with Colonel Olson sending any of the bad ones overseas and keeping the good ones. The effect of that policy is extremely evident over here. The men who came over in '42 and '43 were good, but those who came in '44 were chumps and goof-offs, for the most part. Particularly in this command, the level of officer efficiency has been extremely low, but with new blood coming in, it is improving. We'll get the no-goods culled out by the first of the year. Then build the thing up to a

decent level, and the regulars will be coming out by March, and
I can come home.

Love, D

❖ ⋯⋯⋯ ◆ ⋯⋯⋯ ❖

His practical side still dialogues with Mom about their plans when he
gets home. His emotional side breaks through at time when Mom talks about
Christmas or remembers the beauty of America that he has experienced.

❖ ⋯⋯⋯ ◆ ⋯⋯⋯ ❖

October 19, 1945

My beloved darling,

...So at least we can decide this: We won't know what the
next move is until sometime after I get back. That's not much
help in your planning, is it? But I'll have 78 days' terminal leave
accrued by April 1, 1946. So, in 11 weeks, we should be able to
get readjusted. So do not worry, my wonderful one, just keep
loving me—be patient and I will come to you. Then we will
know what to do.

Love, D

❖ ⋯⋯⋯ ◆ ⋯⋯⋯ ❖

October 22, 1945

My Darling,

...You make me want to cry with your talk about
Christmas. You make it sound so pretty. In a way, I'm glad that
the question is settled even though negatively, because so many
lads are waiting with bated breath to get out on the hope they'll
be with their mamas and kids by Christmas, and so many of
them will be disappointed! But the old Papa will be coming soon

afterward—when the spring comes—the yellow flowers and green bonnets—Easter bonnets and pretty clean streets. Love D

October 24, 1945

Darling,

Places where I've been with you and places still in my memory from years back which we must visit: Cape Cod; an Episcopal Church on the road to Nobska Point lighthouse, with boxwood trees in the churchyard down Woods Hole way; the Maine Coast; Congress Square Hotel in Portland, ME, where from the dining room on the top floor you can see 23 lighthouses; Vermont; Equinox Mountain Inn—just below the mountain— big, white pillars against much green; Litchfield Inn in north- western Conn; the high plains of Kansas; the mountains of Utah and Salt Lake; The balminess of California. The first six months I was away, I missed you so, but now this is a new kind of miss- ing you, a nostalgia—a homesickness for you and all of America, Americans and American places.

Love, D

CHAPTER 19

Dad's Frustration with the Regular Army Management

DAD'S LETTERS (NOVEMBER 1945)

—•••••••••••—•—•••••••••••—

ADMINISTRATIVE OPERATIONS ARE CHANGING RAPIDLY AND almost daily and weekly. Many of Dad's fellow officers are being transferred to various places north of the Philippines, including Japan. Dad ends up being made administrative head of operations. He had hoped that his good friend, Lt. Colonel Glober, would stay on as his co-director of the office in the technical division, but Glober is moved to Okinawa. Dad's replacement, Captain Newland, arrives from the States and it is understood that Dad will train him to take Dad's place. Colonel Maugham is made commanding officer of the entire Far East Asia Services Command and moves to central offices and a new commanding officer arrives in early November. Dad's stable group of officer friends is all now transferred or leaving for home.

—•••••••••••—•—•••••••••••—

November 2, 1945

Darling,

Seeing these people all going home is almost too much to take. I hope they get the hell out of here fast, so we can forget about it until our time comes. It's just too much to have them stand around day in and day out talking about going home. I am particularly exasperated by those who have just come over two or three months ago or even less. But as long as the point system is in effect, that kind of thing will happen.

Love, D

November 9, 1945

My dearly beloved,

Do not be the worrying one because my sickness is just a momentary upset, I'm sure. But I do not like to be sick when my Punkin is not close by to take care of me! One thing, I'm working too hard at the office. You just cannot drive yourself in this climate and these past two days I've been driving to keep ahead while all the folks are away in Tokyo.

My replacement came in yesterday. A Captain Newland, who has been administrative inspector in Hondo, TX, for three years. Very good efficiency ratings and two commendations—looks like he'd be just about ready to take over from me come March or maybe February....

Love, D

The following letter demonstrates the extra mile Dad will still take to help people in the service.

Saturday, November 10, 1945

Darling,

...Today I fixed up four WACS (Women Army Corps) who were left behind when the Surline sailed yesterday. They want to stay to be discharged over here and accept civil service appointments to work in the War Department in Japan. They got all tangled up with administrative difficulties in transferring to the 22nd Replacement Depot to be discharged. Their records all went with the Surline, and they didn't get scratched from the passenger list until after it sailed. They had to radio the ship to scratch them and mail back the records from San Francisco. Everybody over here was just going to let the girls sit and wait till the records got back! So, Poppa went to bat and started checking the 'button' around for the IG button. And building fires under people. As a result, the girls have transferred already from the 22nd to Women's Disposition Center, where they'll be discharged about Tuesday on temporary records and be ready to go to Japan as civilians by next Wednesday!

I have also been trying to help my barracks mate, Major Westbrook, the guy who is in his 47th month overseas. He is administrative assistant to our General, who will not release him. Ridiculous. He's a single guy and the general does not seem to care.

To give you a sense of how fast things are moving, our command had nearly 11,000 men on September 2, VJ Day. On Friday, we were down to 3,421. So, when you look at the thing in perspective, you are amazed that they've moved out as swiftly as they have. But all the world over, the Army is crippled as a fighting machine. If an emergency should arise in the next three or four months, we couldn't do a damn thing but make faces at people.

Love, D

CHAPTER 20

Away from Mom, Dad Battles the Holiday Blues

DAD'S LETTERS (DECEMBER 1945)

◆ ·············◆·············◆

DAD CANNOT BE LIFTED OUT OF DEPRESSION AND JOIN IN
the holiday spirit. He so wants to be home with his Punkin.

◆ ·············◆·············◆

December 4, 1945

Darling Punkin and my Heart's First Affection,

*...For the first time in four years, I'm ready to leave the
inspection business. The new man (commanding officer) doesn't
love me, I guess, and I sure reciprocate. If their pompous brass
hats would only attempt to learn something about the situation—its underlying causes, etc., before they get their minds
made up and start screaming for changes. Well, it's only a couple
of months for real.*

Love, D

❖•••••••••••━•••••••••••❖

December 9, 1945

My dearly beloved,

I haven't written the pretty Punkin for days and days, it seems. Last letter was mailed Thursday morning, I think. But I've been feeling stinky—mentally and physically. Not fit to talk to man or beast. Friday, I goofed off all day—didn't go near the office—had a beautiful time all by myself. Yesterday was only a half-day, so I loafed through it like...laid around all afternoon and evening. Everybody went off to the club to get drunk. But I just sat alone reading on my bunk.

Love, D

❖•••••••••••━•••••••••••❖

December 12, 1945

...I am now officially in the "goof-off" stage. It's common to all grades and all characters about 60 days before leaving. You gradually cease to be worth a damn on the job—until finally you're such a pain they are tickled silly to get you out of the place. That's how I am now. My work is done. Fifty-three days left!

Love, D

❖•••••••••••━•••••••••••❖

December 28, 1945

My darling Punkin,

...It begins to look more and more as I would leave the Army right as soon as I get to the separation center. The business is getting more and more messed up every day. The regular

army is taking over, and each day the asses are getting more and more ridiculous and vicious. Empire-building, up to now, has been picayune compared to what they are doing now. And the revolting excesses of the human comforts and fat-catting taken by the colonels and generals is going to undermine the whole Army. The enlisted men and the commissioned officers are bitter. Not a day goes by but what you hear men say, "When I get out, I'm going to make it my business to see that this Regular Army Officer caste is overthrown, and a new reformation changes the face of the Army." And they are deadly serious. You've seen stories already in the papers about men running for public office on such platforms.

Love, D

* * *

December 31, 1945

To my Dear Jeannie on New Year's Eve,

Happy New Year! Not yet but in a few hours. I feel very dull. Had two whiskey sours before lunch and ate like a horse—am home and read and slept the afternoon away. Had two whiskies and tap winter before dinner. Instead of lifting my spirits and enhancing my appetite, I am more lugubrious than ever. Many of the boys are already whooping it up—many are very quiet. There's another big party at the Officer's Club with a buffet at 1 a.m. However, the spirit at this moment is not inching in that direction, so shall probably be fast asleep by then.

Today came the papers you sent from the Sweeney Institute and I read every word in them.[10] They seemed to kindle a new spirit in Poppa, in me. A desire to get back in Old Sweeney's harness if he wants me. But I'm afraid there won't be

---

10   Where Dad got this master's degree and hoped he might get job after his service.

enough money in it to keep us in the manner in which we want to be kept after all these years of preparation. But in spite of that, these papers have stimulated my desire to get back in the Eastern Pennsylvania local government picture. I would like to be an assistant to Sweeney.

Love, D

●●●●●●●●●●●●●●●━●●●●●●●●●●●●●●

During this holiday week, Dad sent Mom a St. Nick poem that his father had written to him and his brother, Herbie—when they were 10 and 12 in 1916. It is interesting that Grandpa Herb Dunn never wrote one letter to his son Don during WWII that was saved. This makes Dad's sharing of this poem on Christmas 1945 to Mom even more unusual and poignant, especially without explanation.

The poem is written not just to Donald and Herb, but also to two first cousins who had been born by 1916, Alma and Barbara Fones. Barbara dies as a one-year old. It also makes a heart-wrenching reference to Grandpa Herb's oldest son, Kendall, aged 20 in 1916, from his first marriage to Herbie's mother who died in childbirth. All we know is Kendall had left his father's new family in his teens, had become a logger in the Pacific Northwest, and enlisted in the US Army, and was horribly gassed in WWI. Read the poem with all this in mind.

> *To Herbie and Donald: two good little boys*
> > *Your note received requesting toys.*
> *It's nice of you to think of me.*
> > *When time comes around for Christmas tree.*
> *What do you think! The other day*
> > *I took a ride in my big red sleigh*
> *To count the toys that I had made*
> > *For girls and boys of every shade.*
> *I'm sorry now I must confess*
> > *You'll have to get along with less*

Were I to give you everyone?
    Alma and Barbara would have none.
I'm sure had you a drum to play
    Abbie and Pop would move that day
And put me in such vile disgrace
    And pull the whiskers from my face
A cat, a horse, and wagon too.
    Oh! What would mama do to you
When you went driving up and down
    Front stairs, back stairs, all over town.
What worries me at Christmas time
    When the days get dark, the sun don't shine
And the cold white snow begins to fall
    Is th' thousands of kids with no shoes at all.
I hope your brother (Kendall) now far away
    Will come to you on Christmas Day
A fine strong lad with eyes of blue
    May God bless him, and God bless you.
And now my boys a fond good night,
    For when I come, you'll sleep so tight
You'll never know that I have been near
    With my pack of toys and Christmas cheer.
Love,
St. Nick
H. L. Dunn – 1916

CHAPTER 21

New Year Brings the Hope of Sailing Home

DAD'S LETTERS (JANUARY 1946)

◆ ············· ◆ ············· ◆

AS THE NEW YEAR BEGINS, IT BECOMES CLEAR THAT IN ALL likelihood, Dad will leave for Stateside sometime in March. Although he does not have final confirmation, he is clearly focused on his future after he leaves the service. He writes a long letter to his thesis advisor and mentor, Dr. Stephen Sweeney, sharing information about his war service and inquiring about the possibility of a job when Dad returns home.

◆ ············· ◆ ············· ◆

January 1, 1946

Dear Dr. Sweeney,

New Year's Day in Manila. The holidays have been hollow, despite many club parties and chapel programs. But my belly is full and I want to come home and not stay in the Army. The Army gets more intolerable each day. The pious hopes of the War Department uttered in Washington are so traduced by the time they reach the GI in the ranks, as to be unrecognizable. The Regular Army Officer caste is taking over, period. And they go on building empires as fast as they can. But it's more vicious than that. We've got a bunch of autocratic freebooters as 'wheels' in this command, and they haven't heard that the war has ended. At this moment, they are attempting to keep the majority of officers' 60 days beyond the date they become eligible for separation from the service....

Be all that as it may, Jeanne forwarded some routine material sent out by the Institute, and it sent up my ears four miles high in anticipation of returning to the fold. It looks to me as though this in-service training of public officials is the real 'tops' in the program thus far. I mean, it looks like the thing which has exerted the most direct and hardest hitting impact on helping the public official to do his job. Anyway, the various perspectives, bulletins, and reports whetted my appetite for the local government arena in Eastern Pennsylvania. One thing I've been thinking a lot about lately is the possibility of taking a year or two at the Law School. I have no desire whatever to be a lawyer or to take courses leading to general practice. But I would like to get some formal law schoolwork.

I'm enclosing a job description of the two jobs I've had in the Army if it will be any help in your post-war planning.

Jeanne, I believe, plans to be in Philadelphia in January and will doubtless call to pay her respects. I have urged her to see what she can do about finding quarters for us in or around Philadelphia, so we'll have a place to hang our hats at least during the job-hunting period. She has been wonderful during this trying separation and her letters have been a tremendous source of strength to me. We want to settle down and have a dozen kids!

It's been great to have a chat with you. It's been a long time. Accept my very good greeting to all the returning veterans. And Happy New Year to Mrs. Sweeney, to the children, and to you.

Sincerely,
Don Dunn

•••••••••••••◆•••••••••••••

January 13, 1946

Darling,

...This whole discharge and separation thing is a confused mess and no nearer a solution than weeks ago. It shows what happens when an operation is run on fear of punishment—and then when that fear of punishment is removed, the whole thing falls apart and the colonels and generals stand around wringing their hands—screaming what an unruly mob of civilians they have on their hands. Like some colonel last month at a demonstration at one of the Replacement Depots—when the boys had a mass meeting to bitch about no shipping. This fool told them they could not behave like that, they were in the Army, not work for General Motors. Of course, it was picked up by the United Auto Workers in Detroit inside of 48 hours and they made the Colonel look like an ass. Boy, they can be so stupid. They have no more idea of the temper of the country and the people than the man in the moon. Sometimes, I can't understand how we ever won the war, at all.

Love you, Punkin,
D

CHAPTER 22

Going Home

(FEBRUARY AND MARCH 1946)

AFTER THE INSPECTION TEAM COMES BACK FROM THEIR
tour of Tokyo, Dad's commander finally gives him the word that he will be
released to go home.

◆ ············· ◆ ············· ◆

February 23, 1946

My Purtiest Punkin,

*I am coming! I am coming! Yesterday, the boss man gave
me leave to put myself on orders at the most propitious time to
be sure and sail between the tenth and fifteenth of March. So,
Wick and I are going on orders on March 1 and then tell the
Depot to put us in line to sail on the first boat after the tenth.
Thus, we'll do our waiting while we're still working—not have to
wait through hundreds of priorities. The boss man also told me*

*I was his number one man in the office, and he was going to be
very sorry to lose me!*

 Love you, Punkin,

  D

✦ ·········· ➤ ·········· ✦

February 28, 1946

My Dearly Beloved,

 *Instructions have already been issued to put the Poppa
on orders! Now, it is real. I shall have the order is my hand by
this afternoon or tomorrow morning! We go to the Depot Friday
afternoon to arrange to get on the first boat after the 10th.*

 Love,

  D

✦ ·········· ➤ ·········· ✦

March 2, 1946

My Dearest One,

 *It is really true—I am on my way home. I am registered
in at the Depot and actually awaiting shipment to the United
States. I have just sent a cable to you.*

 *'Fort Dix' is the place, April 7–12 is the date, suggest
meeting at any Philadelphia hotel of your choice.*

 Love,

  D

✦ ·········· ➤ ·········· ✦

March 12, 1946

My dearly beloved,

Now it is settled. Wick and I are sailing on the ship, the Admiral Benson, Friday, March 15. Today, I finished my packing. All set now—hold baggage must be at the Depot tomorrow noon. We will load either Thursday night or Friday morning. So, all is well. They say it's one of the largest transportation carriers. 4,735 officers and me. If we leave on Friday, as scheduled, we will be in Frisco by March 30 with arrival in Ft. Dix, NJ, by the first week in April.

Tonight, Mr. Boss had all the officers at the Army-Navy Club for dinner—a goodbye party for the Poppa. Wow! What a wonderful steak! How good! There were 11 of us, two rounds of drinks, a wonderful steak dinner, and some gab. A splendid evening!

Tomorrow night, I'm having dinner with George Glober. Such a wonderful feeling to know that I'll be with my love in less than a month. Love you, Punkin

D

◆ ⋯⋯⋯ ◆ ⋯⋯⋯ ◆

March 13, 1946

My wonderful Darling,

This is the last communique from Pacific Theater from your Poppa! I shall add to it from time to time until we actually leave. The hold baggage is all stenciled and bonded and I'm now waiting for a vehicle to take it over to the Depot. This noon at 13.30 we will have our final physical exam—then at 08.00 tomorrow morning, we assemble for loading on the Benson. She will probably sail Thursday night or early Friday morning. Like all other big events—it doesn't seem true I am actually about to sail. But the time has at last come. I am so happy.

Had a lovely dinner with George Glober at the red tile place that I found during my first few days here—now called Bayside. Also went for a swim in the marble pool. How beautiful it is down there—the foliage and blossoms and after dinner, it was moonlit. If only all of Manila was like this, then I would send for the Little Punkin to come to the Philippines. It's been getting hot and humid now—it will be good to leave it behind and get up in the cold water of the North Pacific. We sail a circular route curving away up to 43-degree N. Everything is ready now for leaving here at 7.30 in the morning to be in the Depot at 08.00.

8:00 am—Friday—NOW IS THE TIME. WE GO. WE GO. I must run now and get on the truck. I'm on the way home.

USS BENSON TROOP TRANSPORT THAT BRINGS DAD
FROM MANILA TO FRISCO

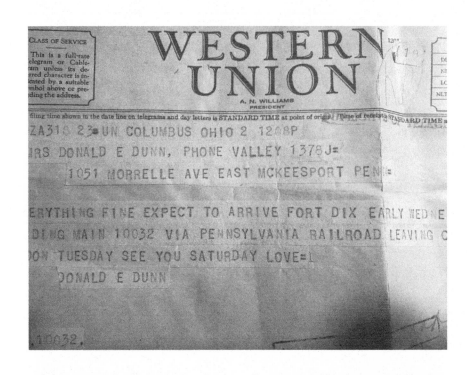

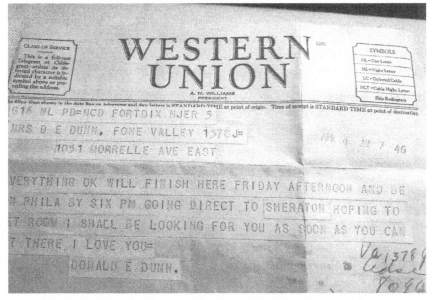

TELEGRAM FROM DAD TO MOM ANNOUNCING HIS ARRIVAL AT THE
SHERATON HOTEL, PHILADELPHIA ON APRIL 4, 1946.

EPILOGUE

MOM AND DAD JOYFULLY REUNITE ON FRIDAY, APRIL 4, 1946. They go on their planned second honeymoon, stopping in Washington, D.C, Monticello, drive the length of the Skyline Drive, and spend some time at Big Meadows Lodge in Virginia.

We do not know the specific details, but they probably drive to Pittsburgh to see Mom's family and up to New London to see Dad's family, as well as seeing friends along the way.

What they find in Connecticut is Dad's father, Herbert Luther Dunn, doing very poorly, suffering from advanced heart disease toward the end of April 1946. Where they go after that is unknown but are called back to New London when Dad's father Herb dies on May 9, 1946. Grandma Leo passes on in 1949 at the young age of 69 after a hard life of running a large household and nursing her father and husband.

Their sadness and grief over his death is softened soon afterward when they discover that Mom is pregnant with my brother Chris. Their job search over the summer of '46 results in Dad finding a job as an assistant professor at the University of New Hampshire, Durham, NH, teaching courses on local and state government. The joy of their time in NH is the birth of my brother, Christopher Schubert Dunn, on January 5, 1947, in a raging blizzard. But after two years there, the salary is just too low for a growing family. Dad returns to state government in Harrisburg, PA, where Jonathan Stephen Dunn (I am nicknamed Timmy by my older brother) was born on January 12, 1950, also on an icy winter morning. They stay there for about four years until my brother Chris and I (Tim) are five and two years old.

In 1952, Moorestown, NJ, a progressive Quaker town just 10 miles from Philadelphia, is looking for a Town Administrator. He is selected and their dream of living in and around Philly comes true. They build a house at 302 Evergreen Drive. Chris starts kindergarten at a newly built Baker School, and we enter into the life of a close-knit community for our growing up years, along with hundreds of other Baby Boomers. Mom and Dad have chosen the more stable route described in some of their war letters as the well-traveled country lane rather than the adventure on the West Coast. Moorestown is a place where we all can put down roots.

After happy childhoods and Mom finding a career path for herself in the public schools, our world is turned upside down 12 years later in 1964, when Dad dies of a massive heart attack. Luckily, Mom has gotten her teaching credentials and she supports the two of us to graduate from Moorestown High School and on to college at Colgate and Haverford College, respectively.

My mom continues to teach business education there until she retires about 1980. Moorestown, in spite of the pain associated with the loss of Dad, becomes the still point in all our lives, a place to come home to, old friends, and mostly fond memories, much like the New London that Dad describes to Mom in the memoir's earliest letter on Christmas Day, 1939.

After trying Florida for two years, she comes back to the Moorestown area until she is 80 years old. With her health and memory failing, she moves to the Boston close to my family, with visits from Chris' family from Ohio. After four years, she suffers a major stroke. Her three grandchildren try to cheer her up, but she passes away in August 1998 and is buried next to Dad in Moorestown, NJ, at the First Presbyterian Churchyard.

Chris and I with our families make various pilgrimages back to Moorestown, most recently, for our 50th high school reunions. As time moves ever forward, we maintain friendships with our high school friends with Christmas cards, emails, and visits around the country, modeling for our own kids the "country lane life with established roots" that Mom and Dad chose for us described in those 1945 letters. Different paths with different goals, but with roots that will last.

We hope this memoir of Dad's and Mom's correspondence, *The Poppa and The Punkin: A WWII Romance Told in Letters (1939–1946),* will keep their romance alive for the coming generations of our family, and the future descendants of the "Greatest Generation."